BOMBS AWAY
BY PATHFINDERS OF THE
EIGHTH AIR FORCE

BOMBS AWAY
BY PATHFINDERS OF THE
EIGHTH AIR FORCE

by

MARSHALL J. THIXTON*
Major U.S. Air Force, Retired

GEORGE E. MOFFAT*

JOHN J. O'NEIL

*Deceased

FNP MILITARY DIVISION
TRUMBULL, CONNECTICUT 06611 USA

Library of Congress Catalog Card Number: 96-62001
ISBN: 0-917678-39-7

Second Printing 1999

Front cover painting and endpaper maps
were done by Ray Bowden

Printed in the United States of America

PREFACE

This book tells the story of a B-17 crew in training in the United States and in combat in the Eighth Air Force in World War II. The combat phase covers missions in a regular heavy bombardment group (95th) and missions in the original pathfinder group (482nd). The missions included the usual multi-plane day missions and special single-plane night missions to Germany.

Initially, Marshall Thixton intended to write the story of his experiences as a bombardier in training and in combat. And thus, the story begins with the early period of Marshall's life in Texas, his joining the U.S. Army Air Forces, and training as a bombardier. However, in writing about combat missions, Marshall decided it would be preferable to expand the story to include the air crew he was a member of and enlisted the aid of George Moffat, ball-turret gunner, who had written accounts of their combat missions soon after their happening, and also John O'Neil, tail and waist gunner. There is also an interesting account of a pathfinder night mission to Germany, which was written by our pilot, Bill Owen.

The authors for the chapters in the book are listed at the beginning of each chapter. For chapters containing contributions by more than one author, the text sections are duly identified as to the author. All other portions of the multi-authored chapters were written by Marshall Thixton.

After arrival in England in late September 1943, Marshall and George and fellow-members of Bill Owen's crew joined the 95th Bomb Group. Both Marshall and George provide interesting accounts of missions to Germany and life on an Eighth Air Force bomber base in this early critical phase of the air war against Germany.

In November 1943, the Owen crew was assigned to the 482nd Bomb Group (Pathfinder), which was the first and only pathfinder group to lead combat missions to Germany using radar and radio beam equipment in the period from September 1943 through March 1944. The Owen crew participated in the first mission to Berlin on March 4, 1944 along with the 95th Bomb Group and 100th Bomb Group, and as the pathfinder aircraft was the first USAAF B-17 to bomb Berlin in WWII. In later March 1944, the 482nd ceased leading bombing missions to Germany, and became a radar training base for navigators/bombardiers/technicians. Future pathfinder missions were assigned to crews trained in pathfinder techniques at the 482nd, and who, along with radar-equipped bombers, were sent to heavy bombardment groups throughout the Eighth Air Force. The 482nd flew special single-plane night missions to Germany in which radar mapping, testing of new or modified radar systems, and the dropping of propaganda leaflets and bombs were carried out until the end of the war in May 1945.

During the 482nd Bomb Group phase, John O'Neil, Harlen Sours and Edmund R. Aken joined the Owen crew as replacements for Bill Galba who died on the Solingen mission, Harry Stotler who was relieved from combat for medical reasons, and Lloyd Cain who was wounded on the Munster mission, and relieved from combat for medical reasons.

When the war in Europe ended in May 1945, the 482nd returned to the U.S., and resumed pathfinder activities at Victorville Army Air Base in California until the war in the Pacific was over in August 1945.

All members of the Owen crew survived combat and returned to the U.S. after the defeat of Germany and eventual discharge from the military.

Unfortunately, author George Moffat passed away in 1993 after battling cancer and other ailments for several years, and author Marshall Thixton died in 1996 from a massive heart attack.

Although there is an excellent book available on British RAF pathfinders, I do not know of any book that tells the story of U.S. Army Air Forces pathfinders, and that is the need we hope this book will fill.

We have attempted to be as accurate as possible and have used throughout the book official USAAF records, actual maps used during missions, other reference sources, and personal diaries and recollections of our crew members.

We have made every effort to obtain permission for the use of photos or other material previously published, and to credit these sources. In the Acknowledgments, we have listed all those individuals and institutions who helped in the preparation of this book.

We sincerely regret any omissions, and would be happy to include such in future reprintings.

It has been a wonderful experience getting back in contact with our former crew members: Marshall Thixton, George Moffat, Bill Owen, Don White and Harlen Sours, after a hiatus of about 45 years. I am glad we have been able to tell the story of one pathfinder B-17 crew in the Eighth Air Force during World War II.

JOHN J. O'NEIL
Trumbull, Connecticut

ACKNOWLEDGMENTS

On behalf of Marshall Thixton, George Moffat, and myself, I wish to acknowledge with sincerest thanks the help and assistance of the following individuals and institutions in preparing this book.

Peter F. Ardizzi, Wilfried Beer, Pat Carty, Cecil Cohen, Richard M. Colegrove, Paul Collins, Trevor Constable, Robert V. Decareau, Kay Engelhardt, Eugene Fletcher, Roger A. Freeman, Samuel A. Goldblith, H.E. Guerlac, Truman Hermansen, Stephen M. Hutton, Edward Jablonski, Helmut Knecht, Leslie Kring, Ed Kueppers, Paul Lathrop, Raleigh D. Lyles, Phoebe Moffat, Mary Moylan, Roger Moylan (Deceased), Eileen Owen, James Parton, J. Piekielko, Mildred Plymale, Leland Pyle, Ron Pyle, Fred Rabo, Lois Ring, O.D. 'Cowboy' Roane, Dennis R. Scanlan, Jr. (Deceased), Harlen 'Hop' Sours, Lorene Thixton (Deceased), William R. Thixton, Cecilia Ann Thixton Toenebohn, Raymond F. Toliver, Michael J. Tully, and Don White.

And the *Boeing Company, Eighth Air Force Historical Society, 457th Bomb Group, 482nd Bomb Group (P) Association, 95th Bomb Group (H) Association, Raytheon Aircraft — Beech Hawker, Smithsonian Institution Press, Time-Life Books, U.S. Air Force,* and the *U.S. Army Air Forces.*

Special thanks are due *Bill Owen,* who helped all of our crew in so many ways during our wartime experiences and especially, Marshall, George and me in the telling of our story in this book. Bill was not only a great pilot and leader, but is one of the finest human beings I have ever known.

We owe a special recognition to my wife, *Lillian,* who typed the original manuscript, and retyped revised manuscript for the book, and was always available to give encouragement, and guidance on editorial questions.

I acknowledge the valuable assistance of our typesetter, *Maureen Yash,* who also helped on questions of style and format, and was a sympathetic listener to my many tales during the several years we worked on the book.

We thank *Ian Hawkins,* renowned author of WWII history, for his generous advice and guidance in getting us started, for his consultations during the writing phase, and his kindness in allowing us to use photos and graphs from his book: *The Munster Raid — Bloody Skies Over Germany.*

We owe a debt of gratitude to *Ray Bowden,* artist, author and publisher, for providing the painting of a pathfinder B-17 for our front cover and the map of Great Britain, Ireland and Europe that is in the endpapers of this book.

If we missed acknowledging the help of any individual or institution, I apologize, as it was unintentional.

JOHN J. O'NEIL

CONTENTS

INTRODUCTION

MARSHALL J. THIXTON

Before any story is told about World War II, a review of events leading up to the war is in order. Beginning in about 1939, as the war started in Europe, the United States began some serious planning on the basis that our nation would become involved. Our country was so divided on many issues that it was almost impossible to do any serious planning or preparation for the coming conflict.

Japan had started in the early thirties on a course of war in the Far East. History records many of the events leading up to the restrictions we took against Japan, but overall, our nation was not very concerned about what was happening in Korea or Manchuria, although our government was concerned about China. All in all, our government's biggest concern was Germany and what was happening in Europe.

The people of the United States could not agree on what action, if any, should be taken. There was a strong isolationist movement against any involvement in European affairs. In the United States a Nazi Party group was pushing for Germany, and the Communist Party was working for the complete overthrow of our government.

President Roosevelt won reelection in 1940 on a promise not to get involved in the European war, although he was working full time on attempting to build up the nation's military capability.

Our relations with Japan were deteriorating because of their attacks on China and finally resulted in an embargo on oil shipments to Japan. To carry on their expansion plans, Japan had to have oil, and this brought on their attack on Pearl Harbor. To ensure an oil supply, the Japanese had to capture Indonesia. To prevent the United States from interfering in this operation, they needed to destroy our navy. They nearly did this with the Pearl Harbor attack. The only thing they missed was our carrier fleet, which slowed down their operations in capturing the needed oil supplies in Indonesia. Their attack on Pearl Harbor indeed awoke a "sleeping giant," as reported by a Japanese admiral, and it united the United States against Japan and Germany.

Americans flocked to the recruiting stations. They came from the cities, from the mountains, and from the heartland. The biggest armada was beginning to be formed. Along with this buildup, it was necessary to speed up the draft, which was already in place. Almost overnight, factories were converted to war production. The speed of total war time production undoubtedly set a record that will never be equaled.

Our story is about the U.S. Army Air Forces, but similar stories could and have been told of the Army, Navy, Marines, and all their units of the Armed Services that became fighting forces in a very short period of time. It has

1

often been said that history repeats itself, but I doubt if ever again this nation will respond as well as it did in World War II.

This story relives the war experiences, including some of the most intense air battles over Germany, through the eyes of three B-17 crew members, Marshall Thixton, bombardier, George Moffat, gunner and John O'Neil, gunner. Diaries and remembrances of fellow crew members add to these experiences.

It is hoped that our story will add to the many skillful works already written by others of the courage and accomplishments of many allied airmen in this period of our history.

For those who are interested in reading more about World War II, there is a good book on the causes and conduct of the war titled, *The Story of the Second World War* by H.S. Commager.

CHAPTER 1

BOMBARDIER TRAINING

MARSHALL J. THIXTON

PART I — THE EARLY YEARS

My early life was a little different than most of my fellow airmen. I was sent to the State Orphans' Home in Corsicana, Texas, when I was about nine years old. I lost my father in a car accident, and my mother was confined to a hospital, so an aunt became guardian of my three younger sisters and me. She could not take care of all four of us and decided to put us in the Home. When we arrived at the Home in 1933, there were over 800 students ranging in age from 5 to 18 years old.

One popular sport at the Home was rabbit hunting, which when successful also provided some good eating. A bunch of 15-20 boys would get sticks and go through the nearby woods looking for rabbits. When a rabbit would jump up, a number of the boys would let loose a fusillade of sticks at the rabbit. Some of the boys were quite accurate with the sticks, and usually a fair supply of rabbits would be taken. Some of the rabbits seemed to learn, however, that if they stayed hidden, they could survive.

I really didn't care much for this sport and usually followed at the back of the line. On one such hunt, I was dragging up the rear and suddenly a rabbit,

FIG. 1.1. MARSHALL J. THIXTON, AT STATE ORPHAN HOME,
CORSICANA, TEXAS IN 1940

apparently thinking he was safe, jumped up and started running to the rear. I threw my stick at him and made a bullseye, breaking its back. As he lay there squealing, I went over to him and finished the job. That was my last rabbit hunt.

I graduated from the State Orphans Home in May 1941. The state furnished each of us with a gladstone bag full of clothes and turned us loose. I had sold candy in the home and had saved $6.50. I was lucky as others had no money and some didn't even have a place to go.

I soon found a job at a nearby primary flight training base for aviation cadets close to Corsicana. I made up my mind then that if I could ever enlist for aircrew training I would. At that time I could not apply because applicants for aviation cadet were required to have at least two years of college. Following Pearl Harbor, the United States was at war with Japan, Germany and Italy, and with the mass mobilization taking place, the Army Air Forces lowered the requirements for cadet training to a high school education, so I enlisted as soon as I could, which was March 10, 1942. I was put on leave as a buck private until they called me for cadet training in May 1942. When I started my cadet career, I bought a diary and used it quite often. Portions of it are included in my description of my early days of training as an aviation cadet.

PART II — BOMBARDIER PREFLIGHT TRAINING

The following includes material from a diary I kept during my aviation cadet training, together with additional material. The title page of the diary read:

MY LIFE IN THE SERVICE — THE DIARY OF
A/C THIXTON, MARSHALL J., "THE TEXAN"

The publisher of the diary in an introduction exhorted every purchaser to faithfully record all events of one's military experiences in one's diary, and to keep all photographs! Never was better advice given, which I was to learn bitterly later, when I failed to keep records. The dates given on text headings were taken from my diary entries.

May 8, 1942 (Date I became an aviation cadet)

    Physical Record -- A/C Thixton
        Weight — 130 pounds
        Chest — Normal — 31" Expanded — 33"
        Waist — 30"

May 8, 1942 to July 12, 1942

We were in a "Tent City" awaiting classification as navigators, bombardiers or pilots. Squadron F is made up of 126 men. We were given a minor physical examination. If no major problems were found, we were accepted for aviation cadet training. However, due to the rapid buildup of all military forces, and especially the Army Air Forces, I was a buck private and on leave until there were openings in the aviation cadet program. I was on leave from March 10, 1942 until May 8, 1942, when I received orders to report to Maxwell Field, Montgomery, Alabama. One of our first assignments was to go through a series of tests, both physical and written.

I'll cover a little of the physical exam portion first. About 25 cadets at a time were told to strip down to our shorts and for the next several hours we went from one exam room to another. Every part of our body was checked starting with eyes and ending with our feet. I have had many other physicals since this one, but never one as thorough as this one was.

I remember as I was going from one checkpoint to another, I noticed one of the other cadets standing in the hallway. As I passed I noticed tears coming down his cheeks, and I asked, "What's wrong?" He replied, "I have been turned down for training because I am color blind. I have passed all other tests with flying colors, but they cannot use me because I am color blind."

At lunchtime I was told to go eat as many bananas as I could hold, because I was one pound underweight (129 pounds). This I did and I passed my next weight check. I barely made it to the latrine, where most of the bananas were deposited.

The next part of the classification test was mainly coordination testing. One test was on lining up two short poles with about five feet of string attached to each pole. The poles would slide along a bed as you pulled the strings. The idea was to line up the poles exactly opposite each other. Sounds easy, but both eyes must be synchronized to do it.

Another test performed was on a board with 24 holes in it. Twelve round pegs were installed on one side of the board. The objective was to turn the pegs over and reinsert them on the other side. As with most tests, the time for completion was fixed. It appeared to be a simple operation, but working as fast as you can, it was surprising how hard it was.

Most of these tests were designed to test how fast the brain and hands could react together. I believe these tests saved many lives when it was necessary for pilots and other crew members to react quickly to emergency situations. Along with the coordination tests, there were the ever-present written tests covering mathematics, history, and the ability to understand what you have read.

I remember working with a cadet who was having coordination problems. Several of his classmates took turns trying to improve his coordination. Something must have gone wrong after he passed his classification exams. His coordination was so off, he had trouble buttoning his shirt pocket. It was a terrible ordeal for him and for us, because we could not help him, and he was released from cadet training.

As it turned out, there was a lot of spare time waiting for our assignments to bombardier school. Between furloughs we were kept busy. There were marching drills, exercises and even kitchen police (K.P.), which entailed working in the mess hall and peeling potatoes, washing pots and pans, and other unpopular duties. There were also many lectures on proper conduct for cadets and at least once a month on venereal disease (V.D.) (sure glad HIV hadn't shown up then). The lectures, along with slides, left terrible impressions, which were so impressive that I did not even want to see a girl for a couple of days.

There were six men in a tent. Our tent included: Bob Saykora from Florida, J.R. Titus from Florida, E.E. Jackson from Alabama, and Cadet Prickett (whose first name I can't recall) from Alabama. They were really fine young men, and I was glad they were all from the South. The Yanks were all right, but they didn't, in my estimation, come up to the standards of the southern boys. This was not a holdover from the Civil War, as I have as many good friends from the North as the South, and besides, I am from Texas.

We moved to another "Tent City" on May 20, 1942, at Craig Field in Selma, Alabama. This was an advanced training field for British air cadets. The U.S. Army training personnel at Selma didn't think much of the British as soldiers or fliers. My observations of the British cadets were they had an untidy dressing code, rather loose discipline, etc., which was the same criticism our ground training personnel had of the U.S. aviation cadets. In other words, we didn't meet West Point standards. Since the RAF won the Battle of Britain and many other battles, I guess the training personnel were wrong on the Brits too.

We had five in a tent at Selma, and we lost Prickett and Jackson. We got another Florida cadet, J.R. Waddell, whom I liked very much. We had a pretty good setup there, and everyone got along fine. I was still hoping to get shipped to Texas as I thought it was the best state in the union, especially when you had a date with one of those pretty Texas girls.

We moved back to Maxwell Field, Alabama on July 9, 1942, after just returning from a furlough. Nobody liked Maxwell Field and we were all glad they were changing the Classification Center to Nashville, Tennessee. We were also hoping that we would not be among those going to Nashville for some more cold storage. We were supposed to move out July 11, '42, to either Santa Anna, California or to Ellington Field, Houston, Texas. I had been in the Army Air Forces for four months and had been on furlough three months out of the four, but wished I had been training all four months.

July 17, 1942

We are at Ellington Field, Texas, by far the best place we have been for overall accommodations and food. I am in a room with Dominic R. Ventres from Worcester, Massachusetts. He was a little late at our departure formation, and I had to go after him and so here we are. I wonder how long we will be together. He is okay and A-1 for a Yankee. I am going to show him a little bit of Texas, if we can get any time off. I hope he likes it, for most Yankees don't. They can't seem to appreciate the beauty of Texas, although they do like the girls.

We went to school for nine weeks at Ellington Field. We studied physics, mathematics, maps and charts, radio code, and a few more subjects. The mathematics and radio code were very hard for me to learn. Physics — I couldn't seem to learn at all. For the first six weeks we wore a green card with our name on it, commonly called a "gig" tag. Gigs were points given for disobeying rules. When you received a certain amount, you had to pull additional duty. After the green card period was finished, we wore a red tag for three weeks, and then a blue tag for three weeks. Hazing of students had been forbidden since early 1942, but some hazing was allowed. Failing grades, combined with "gigs," could and did get cadets expelled from cadet training.

August 25, 1942

I had a chill and went to the hospital. I had a slight case of pneumonia. Just as I had started recovering, I had another more severe attack which almost put me away.

November 15, 1942

Having recovered from pneumonia, which included a thirty day leave to allow full recovery, I was reassigned to Squadron 11, Flight "C", and began classes where I had left off. I failed mathematics and washed out to start all over again. I was assigned the same bunk I started out in on July 17, 1942. I moved in with a new group, and was really depressed. I was considering dropping out and applying for gunnery school. I had my first trouble with another cadet, a short scuffle, because we knew if caught it was instant dismissal for cadets.

January 5, 1943

Today we finished our preflight courses and are moving out tomorrow for bombardier training, Big Spring, Texas.

PART III — ADVANCED BOMBARDIER TRAINING

We arrived at Big Spring Training Field, Big Spring, Texas on January 11, 1943. Big Spring is located in West Texas. It was no stranger to me, because I had spent my early childhood about 20 miles farther west of Big Spring. I remember several wagon trips to Big Spring, on which we would leave early in the morning and arrive back home at Knott, Texas, late at night.

We were tenant farmers and were very close to the edge of where cotton could be grown successfully on dry land due to the low amount of rainfall. We lived there during a long drought period and many Texans and Okies (Oklahomans) moved to California. A famous book and movie, *The Grapes of Wrath*, told the story of this period. Our family had enough rainfall to keep farming, but blowing sand sometimes turned day into night.

At the very beginning of cadet training, I had a bouncy stride, and when we had graded marches (parades), I was often told to get lost until the march was over. Of course, this upset me, and I tried harder to learn to march. Four cadets were assigned to one instructor. Later, I learned that each instructor had eight cadets to train, or two shifts a day. Our instructor was Lt. Richard Fouts. The other three cadets in our group were Herbert Hayes Alexander, James G. Adcox, and James H.W. Williamson.

FIG. 1.2. WORLD WAR II POWERED BOMBARDIER TRAINER
(Courtesy of USAF Historical Research Agency and Smithsonian Institution Press)

At last I saw the famous Norden bombsight. It was truly a great piece of machinery. Cadets attended a three month course, but before bombs were dropped from an aircraft, cadets trained about three weeks on a ground-base cart. The bomb-training cart simulated the conditions of an actual aircraft dropping bombs about as close as you could get without actually leaving the ground. The bombsight was installed on top of an eight foot cart. When the cart was engaged to start a bomb run, it would be aimed at a small "bug" about ten feet away. At first the "bug" remained stationary until we became fairly proficient in hitting the "bug" on each run. There were about ten carts lined up on the hangar floor. On our first runs, the carts went all over the floor and into each other, but the cadets very quickly got things under control, and we could hit the "bugs" on a regular basis. As soon as the cadets had mastered the stationary "bug," the airman trainers started moving the "bug" at the same time the cart started its bomb run. This made the task of hitting the "bug" somewhat harder.

So far I have covered only the training on the operation of the bombsight. The cadets also had plenty of ground school classes, the idea being the better you understood the theory and complete operation of the bombsight, the better bombardier you would become.

Our class trained on the ground cart for about three weeks before we started flying. My diary shows I was struggling with another problem. I had met a young lady, Lorene Lewis, while I was on sick leave during preflight training. We only had a couple of dates, but we both fell in love. Then the letters began about when we should get married, which was a problem many soldiers faced during the war. We finally decided to be married on February 14, 1943. The Friday night before our wedding, Cadets Alexander, Adcox, Schoolcraft, and Williamson got a can of black shoe polish, and made an attempt to paint my privates with the polish. Their reasoning was that if my wife noticed the difference, she would not be a virgin. It was quite a struggle; I really didn't think they would do this to me, but I wasn't going to take any chances. They finally got me down and then backed off before completing their operation. For that, I was thankful.

We were married that Sunday in the Assembly of God Church. My father-in-law, Calvin Lewis, was an Assembly of God minister, and knew the minister that married us. My wife and I had six hours together before I had to return to the base.

After almost a year in the Army Air Forces, I was finally going to get to fly. On February 1, 1943, I crawled into the AT-11 airplane. What a thrill it was. Alexander and I were to be partners. This was the beginning of a partnership that has lasted to this day. The procedure was: first, one would drop five bombs and the other would take pictures of where the bombs landed. Then we would shift positions and the other trainee would drop his five bombs.

FIG. 1.3. MARSHALL AND LORENE THIXTON ON THEIR WEDDING DAY,
FEBRUARY 14, 1943, BIG SPRING, TEXAS

On one mission, Alexander was dropping his bombs and I was taking the pictures. As Alex opened the bomb bay doors to begin his bomb run, something went wrong, and one bomb was released early. I was following the bomb down with my camera, when Lt. Fouts saw me. He yelled at me, "You take a picture of that bomb drop, and you and the camera will go out after it." Lt. Fouts didn't say, but I suspect he would have had a lot of paperwork to do if I had taken a picture of the wayward bomb.

We flew most of our practice missions at 10,000 feet. Bombardiers had to have a circular error under 250 feet in order to pass the course. This was fairly easy if everything went right, but like many endeavors, things did not always go right. The 100-pound practice bombs had a five-pound charge of powder that exploded when the bomb hit and thus marked the point of impact. The rest of the 100-pound bomb was sand. If the sand got damp, it would tend to pack in one end. This would throw the course of the bomb off during the drop. It was a common practice of cadets to claim wet sand if the bomb was very far off course. Sometimes it worked, but most times the airmen keeping the records would not buy this excuse. The cadets dropped between 50 and 60 practice bombs for their scores.

FIG. 1.4. BEECH AT-11 USED FOR TRAINING BOMBARDIERS
(Courtesy of Raytheon Aircraft — Beech Hawker)

According to my diary entry on March 17, 1943, I was scheduled to graduate on April 1, 1943, and become a 2nd Lieutenant in the Army Air Forces. We still had a low level bomb drop from about 500 feet. This turned out to be one of the hardest drops I had to make. Our target was supposed to be a train, and it was set up with makeshift railway cars. The pilot made a couple of passes over the target, but by the time I could see the cars, we would be too far along the track to drop the bombs. The pilot told me he would line up and tell me when to drop my bombs. This he did, and I was never sure if we hit the target.

We had one more mission, a navigation flight using DR (dead reckoning) procedures. It was a non-graded mission and a lot of fun. I did learn that I was glad I was not assigned to a navigation school at the beginning of cadet training.

To give the reader a more complete discussion on what is expected of a bombardier, I am listing below excerpts from the duties of a bombardier as given in the manual for the B-17 bomber.

Accurate and effective bombing is the ultimate purpose of your entire airplane and crew. Every other function is preparatory to hitting and destroying the target. That's your bombardier's job. The success or failure of the mission depends upon what he accomplishes in that short interval of the bombing run.

When the bombardier takes over the airplane for the run on the target, he is in absolute command. He will tell you what he wants done, and until he tells you "Bombs Away," his word is law.

A great deal, therefore, depends on the understanding between bombardier and pilot. You expect your bombardier to know his job when he takes over. He expects you to understand the problems involved in his job, and to give him full cooperation. Teamwork between pilot and bombardier is essential.

Under any given set of conditions — groundspeed, altitude, direction, etc. — there is only one point in space where a bomb may be released from the airplane to hit a predetermined object on the ground.

There are many things with which a bombardier must be thoroughly familiar in order to release his bombs at the right point to hit this predetermined target. He must know and understand his bombsight, what it does, and how it does it. He must thoroughly understand the operation and upkeep of his bombing instruments and equipment. He must know that his racks, switches, controls, releases, doors, linkage, etc., are in first-class operating condition.

He must understand the automatic pilot as it pertains to bombing. He must know how to set it up, make any adjustments and minor repairs while in flight.

He must know how to operate all gun positions in the airplane. He must know how to load and clear simple stoppages and jams of machine guns while in flight.

He must be able to load and fuse his own bombs. He must understand the destructive power of bombs and must know the vulnerable spots on various types of targets. He must understand the bombing problem, bombing probabilities, bombing errors, etc.

He must be thoroughly versed in target identification, and in aircraft identification.

The bombardier should be familiar with the duties of all members of the crew and should be able to assist the navigator in case the navigator becomes incapacitated.

From my diary and other recollections about my cadet training period, it was truly a long struggle, constantly sweating out passing tests, meeting all the requirements, and keeping your nose clean. I recall an incident in preflight training, when one night two of my roommates got into an argument about cheating on tests. They both admitted they had cheated on tests. The tactical officer was standing outside an open window listening to their discussion. The next morning both were eliminated from the cadet program. I sure was glad I stayed clear of that discussion.

FIG. 1.5. MARSHALL J. THIXTON, 2ND LT. AND BOMBARDIER, U.S. ARMY AIR FORCES

The last entry in my diary was on April 1, 1943. I was commissioned as a 2nd Lieutenant in the Army Air Forces. My wife, Lorene, pinned on my silver wings, and I don't know which one of us was the proudest of this honor. I was hoping for a leave, but we were sent immediately to Blythe Air Base, Blythe, California to begin our combat crew training.

CHAPTER 2

COMBAT CREW TRAINING

MARSHALL J. THIXTON

Almost all of the bombardiers in Class 43-5-B (fifth class for 1943, Bombardier Classification) were assigned to the 34th Bomb Group, 2nd Air Force, Blythe, California. The bombardiers, along with other crew members, became the 34th Provisional Bomb Group (H) and were assigned to flying B-17s.

Blythe, California is located in the southeastern corner of California at the edge of the Mojave Desert. The air base was located about 15 miles west of Blythe, well into the desert. It was in early April 1943 and the temperature was already extremely high during the day, but it cooled off rather fast at sundown. Our crew was given several passes into Blythe. The town was located in a valley several feet below the desert with the Colorado River running through the town. When we would leave the base around sundown, we would be soaking wet from perspiration, but as we descended into the valley, it would become cold and we needed a jacket to stay warm. I had a cousin living in Blythe, so I got to see some of the surrounding area. It was a beautiful place at the edge of the desert.

Our crew was quickly formed, except for a navigator, and we started our training in B-17s. Our crew had 2nd Lt. William V. Owen of Columbus, Ohio as pilot. In addition to being the first pilot, Bill was the airplane and crew commander and thus responsible for flying the airplane and seeing that all crew members understood and carried out their respective assignments. Our copilot was 2nd Lt. Frank McAllister of Omak, Washington. I was a 2nd Lt. and the crew bombardier and my home town was Mexia, Texas. The flight engineer was S/Sgt. Don White of North Bennington, Vermont. Sgt. Lloyd Cain who was from Akron, Ohio, was our radio operator. Sgt. George "Bud" Moffat of Grosse Point, Michigan was the ball turret gunner. Sgt. Ellsworth Beans and Sgt. Harry Stotler were our waist gunners. Ellsworth came from Pittsburgh, PA and Harry was from Greencastle, PA. And lastly our tail gunner was Sgt. Bill Galba of East St. Louis, Missouri.

The armament on a B-17 consisted of 50 caliber (actually 0.5 in. caliber) machine guns. The flight engineer, ball turret gunner, and the tail gunner each had twin 50 caliber guns, and the radio operator and the two waist gunners each had single 50 calibers. The bombardier on early B-17s had a single 50 caliber gun. Later, on the B-17-G model, a twin-fifty turret was installed in the nose for the bombardier. The navigator had a single 50 caliber gun, for a total of 11 or 13 guns, depending on the model of B-17. That's a lot of firepower, as the Luftwaffe was already finding out.

These four-engine, long-range B-17 heavy bombers were flown by the U.S. Army Air Forces in England, Italy, North Africa, China, and the Pacific in World War II. The B-17 was a rugged airplane that could and did sustain unbelievable damage and still bring its crew back safely, as will be verified later in this book. The B-17 was powered by four Wright Cyclone radial engines, each delivering 1,200 horsepower. Its supercharged engines could fly at altitudes up to 35,000 feet and deliver about 6,000 pounds of high explosive bombs to a target. These figures were based on single aircraft flights. In combat formation flying of eighteen or more planes in a group, the numbers were somewhat lower.

FIG. 2.1. B-17-E FLYING FORTRESS
(Courtesy of USAAF)

The "twin fifties" in the top turret and ball turret, though controlled by the gunners, operated mechanically and were guided by a Sperry aiming mechanism that allowed the gunner to lock onto enemy fighters and shoot them down with deadly accuracy. The German fighters tried many formations and diversions in their attacks to try and nullify the accuracy of these guns. The single 50 caliber guns were controlled manually by the gunners, making it much more difficult for them to sight on and hit the fast-moving enemy fighters.

For pinpoint bombing, the B-17 carried the then highly-secret Norden Bombsight with which the bombardier could achieve a high degree of bombing accuracy. Beginning in late 1943 in Europe and throughout the remainder of the air war, radar was used in the B-17s for navigation and for bombing when solid cloud cover hid the targets and prevented visual bombing. Radar allowed the B-17s to fly many more missions, especially in bad weather during the winter months. These early radars were not as accurate as visual bomb drops, because they did not allow pinpoint bombing, but it was possible to hit large targets that gave strong positioning on the radar scope.

It is generally conceded that the B-17 was the best U.S. heavy bomber (the B-29 was a very heavy bomber) of World War II, though this has long been debated by B-24 crews. But where B-17s were used for high altitude bombing (above 25,000 feet) it was the best bomber, and it was the one we were being trained to fly.

B-17 groups had been forming and flying to England as fast as the factories could build the planes, and Gen. Hap Arnold could divert them from other parts of the world to the Eighth Air Force. The first crews arrived in England in mid-1942, and the tremendous buildup of groups there put a strain on the English to provide space for airfields and build the bases for the incoming

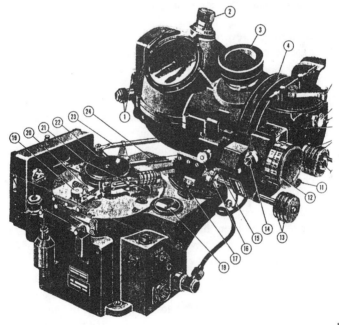

1. Leveling Knobs	13. Turn and Drift Knobs
2. Caging Knob	14. Tachometer Adapter
3. Eyepiece	15. Release Lever
4. Index Window	16. Crosshair Rheostat
5. Trail Arm and Trail Plate	17. Drift Scale
6. Extended Vision Knob	18. PDI Brush and Coil
7. Rate Motor Switch	19. Autopilot Clutch Engaging Knob
8. Disc Speed Gear Shift	20. Autopilot Clutch
9. Rate and Displacement Knobs	21. Bombsight Clutch Engaging Knob
10. Mirror Drive Clutch	22. Bombsight Clutch
11. Search Knob	23. Bombsight Connecting Rod
12. Disc Speed Drum	24. Autopilot Connecting Rod

FIG. 2.2. THE NORDEN BOMBSIGHT DESIGNED FOR PRECISION
HIGH-ALTITUDE BOMBING IN B-17 FLYING FORTRESS AIRCRAFT
Numbers 5-10 are missing from the diagram, but follow in order on the upper
right of the illustration. (From USAAF Norden Bombsight Manual)

airplanes. Some of the new bomb groups had to double up on bases until a base could be prepared for them. The crews and airplanes had been flying to England for nearly a year when we started our combat crew training. No one thought this fast buildup could be accomplished when President Roosevelt said it would be done, and promised Prime Minister Churchill it would be done — and done, it was. The most amazing thing about this operation was that safety was never sacrificed to meet production goals. Of course an operation this big had some failures, but overall, safety was of primary importance and our aircraft failure rate was extremely low. Borrowing a little from one of Churchill's famous speeches, "Never in the history of man did so few crews owe so much to so many men and women who designed, built and maintained the airplanes we flew."

At long last our crew took its first flight in the B-17. I'll give my version of this flight and then my pilot's explanation of what happened. We took off just after it got dark, and it appeared we were flying awfully low as we cleared the runway. In fact, we emptied the officer's club as we passed over it, and I was thinking, is this the way it's going to be? When we landed, I asked our pilot, Lt. Bill Owen, if this was a normal takeoff, and he replied, "It was a dark night with very little runway and confusing runway lighting. I lined up with a long taxiway with plenty of room. Once committed, I continued the takeoff. It was a good lesson and taught me a lot about 'go, no go' situations. You all must shake up easily." All I could say was I hoped this was not going to be a recurring pattern in our takeoffs.

Bill went on to explain in more detail about becoming a pilot of a B-17. "Most of the pilots had been through B-17 transition school prior to being sent to Blythe Air Base. I had not, having been only one month out of flying school and been flying that month as a copilot. My pilot, Dick Brice, gave me extra time in the pilot's seat, including landings. He told me one day to check the bulletin board, and I found I was listed as a first pilot with a crew, for which he had recommended me." I don't know why he told me all of this. I guess it was because it was our first flight, but I do know one thing, our crew could not have been assigned a better pilot, as was proven several times later in combat operations.

Our copilot, Lt. Frank McAllister (Mac), arrived at Blythe under very different circumstances. He was sent to Blythe to stay until a nearby base, being prepared for fighter pilot training, was completed. Since he was at Blythe and they needed copilots, he was assigned to the 34th Provisional Group. Lt. McAllister was one very unhappy pilot. He had trained in T-6s used for training fighter pilots. He was completely convinced he was going to be one of the hottest fighter pilots alive, since his class had won many honors in their T-6 training school. This was such a blow to his pride, that he never fully recovered from it.

One day Bill and I went to the officers' club, where, as usual, Mac was playing poker. He appeared to have had a little too much to drink. Bill and Mac were scheduled for a ground training session in about thirty minutes, and Bill figured Mac would never make it. When Bill arrived at the flight trainer, Mac was already flying the ground simulator and doing one helluva professional job of it. I believe Bill then realized he had an excellent copilot, which also proved to be the case in combat flying later, as long as Bill took care of the small stuff.

The nucleus of a provisional group was formed, and we were transferred to Dyersburg Air Base in Dyersburg, Tennessee. We boarded one of the oldest trains I have ever seen. The conductor said it had belonged to a movie company that had used it in making western movies. Fortunately, we only had to travel in it the short distance to Needles, California. There we boarded a more modern troop train. While coming across Arizona, the train made a refueling stop, and we were told there would be a short delay, but that no one was to leave the train. The major in charge of getting us to Dyersburg said he had trouble on previous trips, and he was not going to allow it to happen to him again. Anyone missing the train would be court-martialed. Four of us decided we would take a chance, and we went into town for a steak dinner. When we returned, the train had already departed. We checked to see when the next train was coming through and found it was not due to arrive until the next day. We knew we were in deep trouble. One member of the four knew enough to send a telegram to the commander on the troop train. He wrote, "FOUR OFFICERS MISSED TRAIN — STOP — PROCEEDING AT ONCE TO CATCH UP — STOP." We had also made a call and found out that the train was scheduled for another stop in Big Spring, Texas. All four of us then started hitchhiking across Arizona. A truck came by and picked us up. We explained our problem to the truck driver, and told him we were in trouble. He said he was going someplace in south Louisiana, but he would take us to Big Spring — the chase was on.

The five of us in the cab of that truck made it awfully crowded, and I suspect it was a long time before that truck driver picked up any more hitchhikers. We made it to Big Spring, Texas, but again our train had already departed. We knew the next stop was in Fort Worth, Texas. Luckily a troop train travels slowly, with several stops to let priority trains go through, so we caught the next passenger train headed for Fort Worth and continued our chase. When we arrived in Fort Worth, we found out from the station manager that our troop train was on a siding. We caught a taxi and told the driver about our dilemma. He gave us a wild ride, narrowly missing several cars along the way, but we made it to the siding and could see our train parked several hundred feet up the track. When we tried to pay the cab driver, he said, "Never mind. It's the least I can do for the war effort." We thanked him and started running after the train. As we got closer, we saw a big puff of smoke come out of the stack and the train started moving slowly. The conductor was standing at the back of the caboose and heard us yelling. He signaled the engineer, the train slowed, and we managed to catch it. The commander must have forgiven us, because he didn't press charges. All I got from Bill Owen was a dirty look.

My wife, Lorene, was planning to come to Dyersburg. Everyone had been told not to bring their wives to Blythe, because there was absolutely no place for them to stay. As usual, a few wives did come, and some had to be put up in the local jail, because that was the only place available. Housing was a constant problem during the war for military personnel and wives, as well as many others.

Lorene arrived in Dyersburg a couple of days before I did. Dyersburg had two nice hotels, but they wouldn't accept unaccompanied women. She found a small hotel that would put her up, but it was one used mostly to entertain local soldiers. It was a busy place twenty-four hours a day. As soon as I arrived at the base, I asked for some time off, so I could go and find my wife and make sure she had a place to stay. I went down to Transportation to see if I could get a ride into town. I talked to a captain, and, as luck would have it, he had helped my wife find a place to stay. He told me to crawl in the jeep and he would take me to her. When I arrived at Lorene's room, it took some time for her to open the door. She had placed everything she could move against the door. I asked her why she had barricaded herself in, and she told me that several soldiers who had a little too much to drink had tried to force their way into her room.

We then went to one of the better hotels and after they checked my ID card and we produced a marriage license, they let us have a room. The hotel management had a time limit of three days, and then Lorene would have to move again. I had to report back to the base, and it was several days before I got off again. In the meantime, Lorene found a place to stay in Halls, Tennessee, a very small town about seven miles from Dyersburg.

Our navigator, Lt. Albert J. Engelhardt, whose hometown was Chicago, joined us and we finally had a full crew. Al was dual-rated, which meant that he had completed both navigator and bombardier training. Such training was often necessary because on twin-engine bombers one person had to perform both duties. Lt. Owen now had a full crew, and we began to form a close bond that was to last a lifetime. We were all in our early twenties except for one "old man," Sgt. Stotler, who was over thirty. I was the only one who was married, and I thought this should entitle me to special consideration. Bill let me get by with it for a short time until it got out of hand, then he took me aside, and explained what he expected from all members of his crew. This turned out to be the beginning of a close relationship that has lasted to this day. He gave me and Lorene all the breaks he could, but I was not to miss any more flights.

One of my bombardier classmates was assigned to the base on a permanent basis. He was given many more privileges than crew members. Crew members were not supposed to leave the base without special passes. My friend had a permanent pass which allowed him to leave the base anytime. He loaned me his pass, and the gate guards, who seldom checked them for details, just waved me on through. Once, when I returned to base, I noticed a line of personnel at the gate, and I knew they were checking passes. I made a quick detour to a hole in the fence I had used before. When I got back on base, I looked up my friend to see what was going on. He told me they had been issued new passes and the guards were told to check every pass leaving and entering the base. Well, it was good while it lasted, but as always in the military, all good things must come to an end, so I returned to using my hole in the fence. Then one night when I returned rather late, the hole in the fence had been mended. I searched the fence for another hole but couldn't find one. It was getting very late, so I went to the gate. The guard on duty called the Sergeant-of-the-Guard, who escorted me to the guardhouse. Once more, however, my luck held; the sergeant knew me, and

FIG. 2.3. OUR CREW AT DYERSBURG, TENN., MAY 1943
Front row, left to right: Lt. Marshall Thixton, Bombardier, Lt. Bill Owen, Pilot, Lt. Frank McAllister, Copilot, Lt. Al Engelhardt, Navigator; Back row, left to right: Sgt. Harry Stotler, Waist Gunner, Sgt. George Moffat, Ball Turret Gunner, Sgt. Lloyd Cain, Radio Operator, S/Sgt. Don White, Engineer, Sgt. Ellsworth Beans, Waist Gunner, and Sgt. Bill Galba, Tail Gunner.
(Courtesy of Bill Owen)

after a strong reprimand, he escorted me back to my barracks. It was getting close to the end of our training, and we were preparing to make our next move, so I didn't make any more trips to see Lorene.

We were kept fairly busy flying, and we had a chance to see a lot of the area around the Mississippi River. The crew was learning to work together as a team. During WWII, the Army Air Forces stressed the team concept constantly to both air crew and ground personnel. We also had ground training, learning more about the capabilities of the B-17s. We learned to fire our 50 caliber guns on moving targets from ground positions in several training sessions. Finally the big day came for me, when I got to drop some 100-pound practice bombs from the B-17. These practice bombs were painted blue and referred to as "blue devils." The bombardier instructor from the base flew with us and wanted to drop the first bomb. He proceeded to drop it almost perfectly on top of the "shack" which was our target. I asked him if he wanted to drop another one. He replied, "Hell, no. I just wanted to show you how easy it was." I took over and luckily my bombs dropped in the general area of the "shack," which made me feel good.

Our training molded us into a smooth running machine. Of course, this was the purpose of much of our training. We had very few crews that couldn't or wouldn't adjust to the situation, as was probably the case in all operations. That's one reason we developed one of the best fighting forces the world has ever seen.

At the completion of training in late July, we were given a short delay enroute and told to report to Grand Island, Nebraska. At the end of my leave, I almost fouled up again. I caught a flight in a trainer plane (a BT-13) leaving Fort Worth and headed for Oklahoma City. The BT-13 developed engine trouble and our flight was delayed. We finally did make it to Oklahoma City, and I caught a train that took me on to Grand Island, Nebraska — one day late.

Major Snow's Provisional Group, which we belonged to, was sent to Grand Island, Nebraska to pick up new B-17s; then we were going to an unknown destination as a group. When we got to Grand Island, the delivery of B-17s was behind schedule, and there were no planes for our group. As Grand Island was a temporary base in the pipeline of bomber crews, we sadly realized that we would soon leave there without a B-17. Our crews had a few days of free time while orders and transportation were arranged for the next move.

One night Bill, Mac, Al and I went to a pool hall in a seedy part of Grand Island. While we were having a beer and watching the pool game in progress, Mac decided to challenge the winner to a game of 8-ball for $20.00. From Mac's experience working in the logging fields of the state of Washington, he was very familiar with pool halls, poker and drinking, so we felt Mac knew what he was doing. Everyone in the pool hall crowded around the table as Mac, with a drink in hand and a cigarette in his mouth, proceeded to break the rack, hole his balls and the 8-ball without a miscue, and collect his winnings. I know we were all glad, except Mac, when we got him out of that pool hall and we headed back to base.

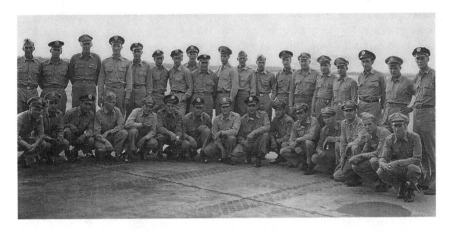

FIG. 2.4. THIRTY-FOUR PILOTS OF THE SNOW PROVISIONAL GROUP AT GRAND ISLAND, NEBRASKA, AUGUST 10, 1943
Lt. Bill Owen is standing number eight from the right. Most saw action in the Eighth Air Force.
(Courtesy of Bill Owen)

Our orders arrived to proceed by troop train to Presque Isle, Maine, which was a holding base for crews being ferried to overseas destinations. The civilian crews were made up of two pilots and a navigator. I never understood this operation, as our pilots had more flying time in B-17s than most of the ferry pilots, and the ferry crew had to be flown back to the states to pick up another plane. When anyone in the higher echelon was asked about this, they had a standard answer, "you don't understand the system." One of these "birds" had the nerve to tell me, "yours is not to reason why, yours is to do or die." I am sure he never made combat, but I hoped a brick would fall on his head. I guess it wasn't necessary for us "peons" to understand the system, since we won the war, but I still think winning the war happened in spite of "the system," or by overcoming "the system."

Once more we were put on standby until sufficient planes and civilian crews were available, and thus, more free time was available. Somehow, I just couldn't handle free time. I became friends with another "Texan" from San Antonio, who was in charge of shipping the combat crews overseas. He also had a car, and together we saw some of the sights around Presque Isle. On one trip, we went across the border into Canada, and I got to eat my first lobster. Of course, it will never replace a Texas steak, but it was good eating.

I told my friend from Texas that our crew would like to go to New York City to see the sights. Presque Isle was a small town, and the girls were very friendly, but there weren't enough to go around. I thought a trip to New York City would solve that problem. Bill, as usual, decided he had better stay put, but Mac, Al, and I decided to go. My friend said he would pull our cards, so we wouldn't miss the flight over to England. However, he only pulled the cards of the three of us, leaving Bill's and the rest of the crew's cards in the file.

My friend gave us the name of a female to contact at one of the plays we were going to see. All three of us went to the theater and arranged dates for after the show. The girls wouldn't be off until eleven that night, so I took off on my own to visit a girl I had been writing letters to since my cadet days. This turned out to be a big mistake. The girl knew I had become engaged to Lorene through my letters, but she didn't know we had married, and I didn't tell her. We had a nice visit and went to a play by ourselves. I found out she had become engaged, and since both of us were engaged, which was her understanding, she felt it best to leave it at that. What I forgot to do was tell her not to say anything to Lorene about my visit. Lo and behold, she wrote Lorene a letter telling about our visit and how glad she was that we had become engaged. It was a good thing I was on my way overseas, and eighteen months would elapse before Lorene could lay her hands on me.

As part of our return trip to Presque Isle, we took a flight to Boston, but soon after we arrived, bad weather set in and we couldn't get a flight out. We decided to wait a day or so for the weather to clear. When it didn't clear up, we took a train to Presque Isle by way of Bangor, Maine. When we arrived in Bangor, we found that the train to Presque Isle was delayed and we had to wait. When we finally did arrive in Presque Isle we found that the rest of our crew had already departed for England. Here we were again, chasing our crew — this time across an ocean. Interestingly, the pilot who ferried us from Presque Isle to England was a "Texan" from Abilene. I had worked for his brother before I entered the service. We had a lot to talk about during the trip.

A scary thing happened on the flight from Presque Isle to Newfoundland for Bill Owen and our other crew members, when the civilian pilots left the cover on the pitot tube (air speed indicator), and the air speed could not be determined on an instrument landing. In spite of this serious goof, the civilian pilots with Bill's help made a successful landing.

We finally caught up with Bill at a staging base near London. The base was used for combat orientation and instruction on how to get along while we were in England. Bill and the rest of the crew had already completed this phase, but they were allowed to stay until we were processed. We finally got it all together, and I feel things turned out for the best, because as a team we saw much of the real war over Germany, and I don't think we would have survived, had we not been a very good team.

CHAPTER 3

AIR COMBAT: 95TH BOMB GROUP (H)
BREMEN — MARIENBURG — MUNSTER — SCHWEINFURT

MARSHALL J. THIXTON
GEORGE E. MOFFAT

Our crew departed the staging base at Bovingdon for our assignment to the 96th Bomb Group. We were only there a few days when we were sent with eight other crews to the 13th Combat Wing, presumably because of the high losses they were having. The 13th Wing sent us and another crew to the 95th Bomb Group; one crew went to the 390th Bomb Group, and five crews to the 100th Bomb Group. One of these 100th crews was piloted by Lt. Rosenthal whose crew in less than two weeks, would be the only one of the 100th to return safely from the Munster mission.

The 95th Bomb Group (H) was located at Horham, Suffolk. The (H) meant that the 95th Bomb Group was a heavy bombardment group which was reserved for B-17s and B-24s. The other designations were medium and light bombardment groups and very heavy bombardment for B-29 groups. Upon arriving at Horham, we were picked up in a G.I. truck for the short ride to the 95th base. The driver of the truck went out of his way to take us down a taxi strip. The taxi strip was used to store damaged B-17s that were mortally wounded on previous missions. We passed one that had the nose section completely blown off. The nose section of the B-17 is where the navigator and bombardier sit. Al Engelhardt (our navigator) and I glanced at one another and shook our heads, wondering if we would be replacing that crew. The driver then proceeded to our barracks area which was located a short distance from the airfield.

An aide then took us to the Nissen Hut. The aide entered the hut and went over to a window and pulled back the blackout curtain. He did not want to turn on the lights, as other crew members were sleeping. As we entered, a crew member raised up in bed and caught my eye. He asked, "Don't I owe you $5.00?" His name was Bob Wing, and he was a classmate of mine in Bombardier Preflight Training (42-18). More about this classmate later on. The aide proceeded further down the hut until he came to four bunks that had their mattresses turned back. We fully realized then that we, indeed, were a replacement crew.

Mission No. 1 — Bremen, Germany (October 8, 1943)
The Following Account Was Written by Lt. Marshall J. Thixton

Lt. Bill Owen had flown a mission on October 2, 1943 to Emden, Germany. He flew as copilot with another crew to become familiar with the procedures he would use when he started flying his own crew. The 95th Bomb Group records show that the 95th lost one aircraft on this mission to Emden.

On October 8, 1943 we flew our first combat mission to Bremen. Although there were no losses by the 95th, 16 planes of the 95th suffered battle damage from flak and enemy fighters. The word "flak" quite appropriately is derived from a German word and was the term used by allied airmen to describe the exploding shells of antiaircraft guns shot by German defense crews from ground emplacements. The German antiaircraft batteries were most numerous around cities, and American and British airmen always had to fly through flak barrages during the actual bomb runs. A direct hit by an antiaircraft shell could readily blow a bomber out of the sky. The exploding 88mm and 105mm antiaircraft shells literally filled the skies with hot metal fragments that could cut through the airplane and kill or wound airmen or damage the airplane. Although the exploding antiaircraft shells were visible as large puffs of black smoke, and when close enough could be heard as a loud whomping sound during the explosion, the hot metal fragments could not be seen until they made contact with the plane or personnel. For this mission a total of 23 B-17s took off. It was standard operating procedure to have several extra B-17s take off in case any of the regular 18 planes scheduled for the mission had to abort the mission because of mechanical problems. If not needed, the extra planes would leave the formation at the English Channel and return to base.

FIG. 3.1. REPRESENTS ONE OF THE EARLY FORMATIONS TRIED IN COMBAT
Each B-17 carried a bombsight, but use was limited since course was set by the lead aircraft. This formation did not give accurate bomb drops, and did not provide a good defense against fighter attacks.

During the mission, I recall that a formation of B-17s ahead of us was under enemy fighter attack and one German Me-109 fighter flew head on into a B-17. Both planes exploded and no parachutes were seen. Our formation flew through the smoke of the explosion and our crew saw firsthand the results of what is an airman's nightmare — the dreaded airplane collision. We were thankful for surviving our first mission, while still realizing there would be 24 more missions needed to complete the then 25-mission tour.

Little did we realize that this Bremen mission was the first of four missions that were to be known as the Black Week Missions. We flew all four of these missions.

A very good account of this mission by our ball turret gunner, George Moffat, follows.

The Following Account of the Mission to Bremen, Germany, October 8, 1943, Was Written by S/Sgt. George E. Moffat

On Thursday evening, October 7th, we were down at the Non-Commissioned Officers' Club eating sandwiches and playing cards. Someone was pounding on the old dilapidated piano; "Pistol Packin Mamma" was the tune. Tobacco smoke filled the room and there was talk of previous missions or hometowns. I was munching slowly on a corned beef sandwich and gazing at some combat photos on the wall and wondering what it would be like tomorrow. We were scheduled for our first mission in the morning. Would I be scared? I knew I was going to be, because that happened to everyone, but would I stand the test of fright? Would I turn yellow? I didn't think so, but anyway tomorrow would determine that. I decided to go back to bed, as they would wake us up about 2 A.M.

Someone was shaking me when I awakened. It was Jazz, the Charge of Quarters. I bounced out of bed. This was it by God! Ellsworth Beans, Don White, Lloyd Cain, Harry Stotler and Bill Galba were already dressing and discussing the possibilities of our first mission. Some of the remarks were quite pessimistic, and I contributed my two cents worth. Beans wanted my blouse and I wanted Whitey's footlocker if in the event one or another of us didn't make it back.

Someone hollered that the trucks were waiting, so we buckled on our Colt .45 semi-automatic pistols and lit a cigarette as we stumbled out of the barracks and up the pitch-black lane. It was 2:30 A.M. We climbed into the truck and tore for the mess hall. Inside it seemed more friendly and warm, as we made bets on the target for today, and ate a special mission breakfast of fried fresh eggs, bacon, toast and strong coffee.

After breakfast, at 3:30 A.M. we went down to the briefing room and got our equipment out of our lockers, checked the electric cords in our heated suits, the carbon dioxide capsule in our Mae West life preserver, and sat around smoking until 4:30 A.M. when briefing began. Major F.J. (Jiggs) Donohue was briefing us. He was the type of man you got courage from, before leaving on a mission. He was confident, cheerful and seemed to have all the faith in the world in "His Boys." I felt better, just listening to him. He finally unveiled the target map and everyone yelped and groaned. It was Bremen! I heard someone next to me swear and say something about "Little B." God-damn. Major

Donohue told us there were 250 flak guns there and 350 single- and twin-engine fighters within a 150 mile radius of the city. Even to me that sounded like one hell of a lot of opposition and I groaned along with the rest of the gang. Beans said, "Well old boy we've had it." He said that on every mission we made.

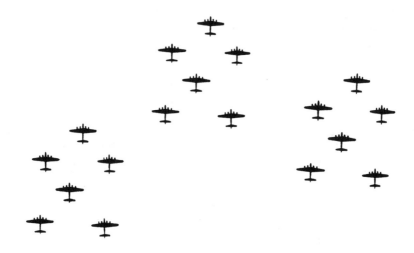

FIG. 3.2. STANDARD EIGHTEEN B-17 FORMATION ADOPTED IN MID-1943
The group of planes in the center is the lead squadron. The right group is the high squadron which flies 200 feet higher than the lead squadron. The left group is the low squadron which flies 200 feet lower than the lead squadron. The outside plane in the low squadron is "tail-end Charlie." This formation was credited to then Col. Curtis E. LeMay.
Three groups comprised a wing, usually of 54 planes, with a lead group, a high group and a low group in similar positions to the makeup of squadrons within the group formation. An air division was made up of a varying number of wings, depending on the number of groups and bombers that were available.
An important point in formations was the rotation factor, wherein bomber crews were rotated in position within the squadrons, and the squadrons within groups, and the groups within wings, and the wings within divisions. Pilot Bill Owen feels the luck of the draw insofar as a crew's position in the formation was an important point in surviving enemy fighter attacks.

After briefing we loaded our stuff on the truck and went out to our B-17. We got our guns out of the armament shop and installed them. After putting on our heated suits, we sat under the wing, smoking and wondering what in blazes we were really up against. At 7:30 A.M., we started engines and at 7:45 taxied out in line for the takeoff. I stood in the radio room and could see the ships all lined up. They sure were a grand sight. Crowds of mechanics and other ground-crew personnel, and Red Cross girls stood at the side, sweating out our takeoffs. We were carrying 10 high-explosive 500 pounders.

Finally our turn came to take off and the engines roared as we picked up speed. It seemed ages before she became airborne because of the weight of the bomb load. We roared over the end of the field and began climbing for altitude. We were off. I felt very much relieved somehow. I was actually looking forward to the mission now.

At 25,000 feet altitude, we made our formation. I was sitting in the waist with Harry Stotler and Ellsworth Beans. At that altitude I was using a walk-around oxygen container. After meeting the other bomb groups, we left the English coast on time. I crawled down in my turret, closed the door and plugged in on oxygen, hooked up my mike and earphones and checked in, "ball turret, OK." Then made my adjustments on my Sperry gunsight and waited. Out over the channel, I test-fired my guns. They worked fast and good. I still wondered what we were getting into and how I would react when the shooting started.

I looked out at 12 o'clock and saw for the first time, the enemy coast. It looked bleak and barren from that altitude, and my spine tingled with excitement. As we passed over the coast I saw 2 or 3 puffs of flak. So that's what it looked like, black, oily puffs with a crimson flash in the center. They were quite a way off and I watched them with interest.

A group of P-47s were escorting us part of the way, and way out I could see vapor trails from them several thousand feet above us. I felt better. I never lost that feeling of security when those boys were around. They saved us many times, but that will come later. About 100 miles from the target, the P-47s left us because they had reached the outer limits of their range, and they were no sooner out of sight than we were jumped by enemy fighters: Me-109s, Focke-Wulf 190s, and Me-110s, mostly. I watched them swarm around for a number of minutes and I was scared, and confused. I was more intent on watching them approaching than shooting, for a few minutes only though, and then as if everyone had been doing the same thing, our crew began to function. Fighters were being called out at all angles of the clock. I blazed away and smelled the powder smoke. It smelled good and I felt good too, though still scared a lot.

The fighters after their initial few attacks then went out to about 2,000 yards, out of our range and some of the crippled Forts fell back. Then the fighters would all jump one crippled Fort. I was so mad I saw red. Some of the Forts back of the formation caught fire. I saw 2 or 3 parachutes come out as the fighters swarmed over them, and the chutes floated gently down. I wondered what was in store for those poor beggars.

Then I turned to 12 o'clock and my mouth dropped open and my eyes nearly popped out. The sky was absolutely polluted for miles with flak shells bursting. So this was combat! My God! I was renewed with fright. I couldn't see how we could possibly get through that barrage. The sky was absolutely black.

FIG. 3.3. GERMAN AIR FORCE COMBAT UNITS, GERMANY AND
OCCUPIED EUROPE, OCT. 1943
(Courtesy of Ian Hawkins)

The group ahead of us was already in it and suddenly I saw a black streak come down and crash into one of the Forts. It made a terrific explosion with all those bombs in her yet. It must have been an enemy fighter whose pilot had misjudged his attack. We flew through the black smoke that had erupted, and then we were in the flak. Flak kept bursting all around and under us angrily, some coming so close it would lift me off my seat. I tried to make myself smaller and hide, but there was no place to hide. I waited for some of that hot steel to come ripping through my turret, into me. I could hear it pinging on the fuselage. The bomb-bay doors began to open. Flak was making the ship jump and groan, then I heard Marshall Thixton say, "Bombs Away." What a relief that was. I followed the bombs down and watched them hit the ground and explode. Columns of smoke rose up toward us. We were still in the flak and ships were going down, burning, wings off, broken-in-half. A few chutes floated down. It was an awful sight.

FIG. 3.4. B-17s ON A BOMBING RUN UNDER A HEAVY FLAK ATTACK
(Courtesy of 457th Bomb Group via 8AFHS and J. Piekielko)

As we left the flak, I took my first (I believe) breath for 30 minutes, and then in came more enemy fighters again. And again the sky was filled with tracers, 20 mm puffs of exploding cannon shells from enemy fighters, falling fighters and burning and crippled Forts. They hounded us intermittently all the way back until we once more met our P-47s. The enemy fighters disappeared as if they had been but a bad dream. I could see many holes in our B-17 even from my position, and although we didn't appear to be hit anywhere seriously, we had certainly been hit heavily everywhere.

When we landed we tumbled out and kissed the old ground. If that's what missions were like, we didn't like them. We counted 134 flak holes in our B-17, two of which were in my turret. We went to interrogation, chow and cleaned our guns. We then fell in bed so very tired. Only 24 more missions to go to complete the tour of 25 missions, and go back home. I found out what I wanted to know. I wasn't yellow. I was already looking forward to tomorrow's mission. I was really glad to know that, for I had wondered about it a lot. It's difficult to say how any man will react in combat.

Mission No. 2 — Marienburg, East Prussia (October 9, 1943)
The Following Account Was Written by Lt. Marshall J. Thixton

This mission was the second longest mission scheduled to that time for the 8th Air Force with an estimated flight time over eleven hours. Our crew manned one of three B-17s from the 95th Bomb Group which would fly with the 100th Bomb Group. The 100th Bomb Group had suffered serious losses in previous missions, and the 95th Bomb Group sent three B-17s to help the 100th complete their eighteen-plane group formation. Of course, the 100th assigned us to the low squadron, and our crew was flying "tail-end Charlie," which was the outside position of the low squadron's last element. See Fig. 3.2 for the tail-end Charlie position of the eighteen-plane formation. Tail-end Charlie was considered the most dangerous position in the formation from the standpoint of the fighter attacks, but as this was only our second mission we did not fully understand this basic fact of air combat. We did after this mission.

The formation headed north over the North Sea at 10,000 feet, as we wanted to conserve our oxygen supply as long as possible. It was standard procedure that oxygen be used by all crew members when the altitude of the plane was over 10,000 feet. The 1st and 2nd Air Divisions were scheduled to hit targets in Anklam and in the Gdynia and Danzig area of occupied Poland, and our 3rd Division hoped that the other divisions would attract most of the German fighters. Evidently, it worked and we saw no enemy fighters on our way to Marienburg, and not until we passed Poland on our return route.

The 100th Bomb Group was carrying 100-pound incendiary bombs to unload on the Focke-Wulf airplane factory, but something went wrong, and we dropped our fire bombs in a wheat field several hundred feet from the target. I am not certain, but I suspect the lead bombardier left his extended vision on his bombsight. By using extended vision in the bombsight, one could see 20 more degrees ahead on the bomb run; however, if you did not remove this 20 degrees as you approached the target, your bomb drop would be 20 degrees off target. This happened to me once on a training mission. In any case, the bombs started a good fire in this wheat field. This was verified later by an American POW (Prisoner of War) in a nearby compound who with others were enlisted by the German guards to fight the fire. The POW said the German guards were very angry at them and made the remark, "The damned Americans were trying to starve us out of the war."

However, the assessment of the bombing of Marienburg indicated that 58 percent of the bombs fell within 1,000 feet of the target and 83 percent within 2,000 feet. The Focke-Wulf fighter factory was almost completely destroyed, and General Eaker described the mission as "the classic example of precision bombing."

As the 100th Bomb Group departed the Danish coast on our return trip, we were several miles out over the North Sea, when we were attacked by German Me-109 and twin-engine Ju-88 fighters. The fighters laid back just out of the range of our .50 caliber guns and lobbed air-to-air rockets and cannon fire into our formation. Most of the German fire was directed at us in the low squadron. The B-17 on the inside of our three plane formation took a hit and slowly left our formation. It went down in the North Sea. We realized that only a German naval ship could save them, if one were close by. The entire crew was reported KIA (Killed in Action). The bombardier on that ill-fated B-17 was my classmate, Lt. Bob Wing. He was a good friend, and as far as I know, our first classmate killed in combat. Our crew had arrived about a week before October payday and Bob added another $20.00 to his bill. On payday I met Bob leaving the officers club and as he saw me he was smiling that outstanding smile. He said, "You'll have to wait until next payday, I was just wiped out." He loved to gamble and I am glad he got a little pleasure out of his short life. The first classmate of mine to be killed was lost on a training mission in Dyersburg. His crew had just taken off on a training flight and crashed and burned about a mile from the air base.

The Following Account of the Mission to Marienburg, East Prussia, Oct. 9, 1943, Was Written by S/Sgt. George E. Moffat

We were all very tired and still cramped from yesterday's mission to Bremen. Last night after we came back to the barracks, we discussed what we had seen that day and our individual reactions. It seemed that they were quite similar in that we had no idea what air combat would be like, and therefore had nothing to compare our feelings with. The same as trying to tell how far a cloud is away from you. We were told that our first mission was considered quite a rough one, so that is what we used as a basis for our judgments of future raids. Anyway, we thought it was rough before even discussing it with anyone.

About 11:00 P.M. things had quieted down and we were contemplating sleeping for what we knew would be an all-too-short time. It was. At 1:30 A.M., Jazz, the Charge of Quarters, came in. I was sound asleep. They had to roll me out. When I finally woke up someone was waving a .45 pistol at Jazz, and threatening to wake him up in hell when we got there. Poor Jazz swore he would never disturb us again as he stormed out the door in great haste. Everyone laughed sleepily and I lit a cigarette and dressed. We went out to the waiting truck, climbed aboard and went up to the mess hall and had that good old pre-mission fresh eggs and bacon breakfast. I thought what an ungodly hour to eat breakfast. I was stiff and I still ached from yesterday's mission. There was a two-day stubble of peach fuzz on my face that only made me feel more uncomfortable. We were certainly in combat now. Up to our rosy necks.

After breakfast we went down to the briefing room. As for our previous mission, we had more than ample time to gather together our equipment, but I didn't spend my time smoking. I fell asleep on a pile of Mae West life preservers almost immediately, and slept until Beans kicked me awake at 4:00 A.M.

We walked into the briefing room and Major Jiggs Donohue was at the table. We sat down, lit up and waited. He began by removing the target cover and my eyes almost popped out. The damn route ran nearly off the map. Over in East Prussia. Good heavens! It must be a shuttle raid to Russia we figured. But no, there was the route back also. I groaned. What a run this would be! When we were told that our altitude was going to be 12,000 ft, some openly declared that it was suicide. It seemed that way to me too, but what could be done about it? Beans came out with his cheerful, "We've had it," as usual, and this time I was inclined to agree. Our mission course was nearly all over water, which was some relief. The problem was though which is worse, to be shot at a little more on a course over land, or be shot at less over water, but have to worry about a ditching in an icy, choppy sea where survival time is about 30 minutes? I was so tired I didn't care particularly, and neither did the rest of the crew.

Jiggs said that the flak would be nil and not too many enemy fighters would chance being shot down over water, so with the exception of it being the second longest run the 8th Air Force had made to date, it should be fairly easy. The gasoline load for each B-17 would be at the maximum, for we needed every drop we could carry. Major Donohue wished us luck and we filed out, picked up our equipment and hopped a truck for the ride to the ship.

When we got off, Pete, the armorer was waiting to see if I needed any help with my turret. I said, "no thanks," and trudged off for the armament shack to get my guns. After cleaning and setting them, I tossed them wearily on my shoulder and came back to the Liberty Belle. She looked ghostly but beautiful in the half light. She sure was a "good girl." Ed, the ground crew chief, led me around to her nose and pointed to the number four engine. I grinned happily. There in yellow paint on the cowling was "Billie Lee." He grinned and said, "I hope that neither the engine nor she gives out while you're flying her." Then he backed off and ran as I aimed a solid foot toward his retreating posterior.

As I was putting my guns in the ball turret, I noticed Willie (my good luck charm) was not hanging in its place and remembered I had left him on my shelf in the barracks. I hailed a jeep and he took me down to get him on the double. I just couldn't go without him.

At 7:15 A.M., we started engines and Don White, Bill Galba and I tossed away our cigarettes and climbed aboard. At 7:30 we taxied out of the hardstand and up the perimeter track toward the runway. At 8:00 the first ship took off, and as we turned onto the runway I saw the "Impatient Virgin" behind us with

Schillinger and his crew in her. Some "Virgin" I thought, with 10 men in her already. The engines roared and we began moving faster and faster down the runway. We were carrying 40 100-pound incendiaries which were napalm bombs. The ship smoothed out as we lifted off near the end of the runway, and we were off on our second mission.

For this mission, our crew was assigned, with two other 95th Bomb Group crews, to fly with the 100th Bomb Group, which was having trouble getting enough planes airborne due to losses. The worse thing about it was we got the "tail-end Charlie" position in the formation.

After rendezvousing with the other bomb groups of our wing, we proceeded on our way. At the English coast I got into my turret and checked everything over again, test-fired my guns and relaxed as much as I could. No one was on oxygen. We were at 12,000 ft and we decided that only if we were subject to attack would we go on oxygen, to make our minds function more clearly. And occasionally take a whiff to keep from getting logy, or we wouldn't have enough in case someone was wounded and needed pure oxygen. It wasn't cold enough to plug my heated suit in, as it was heavy enough and kept me warm for quite awhile.

It seemed much longer than it actually was before we even reached the coast of Denmark. We had an acknowledgment of our being present in the form of 3 or 4 bursts of flak that wasn't too accurate anyway. We shot the bull over the intercom and tried to keep our minds off of the 12,000-foot bombing altitude as much as possible. Once over Denmark, we started out over the Baltic Sea and I was feeling cramped already, having been in the turret for 2½ hours. It was about two hours later that we cut southeast and began heading inland for Marienburg. I was aching all over. I had plugged in my heated suit to help my circulation somewhat.

As we approached our target, I put on my oxygen mask and slipped on my gun switches. At our 12,000-foot altitude, we expected to get shot to the devil by both heavy and light flak. At 12 o'clock, I could see columns of dense smoke rising nearly to our altitude from the target area. The first wave of Forts were carrying demolition bombs. Our bomb-bay doors came open and I whirled my turret around and around searching for the expected enemy fighters, but the sky was clear, except for Fortresses. Flying tail-end Charlie in the Purple Heart corner makes you wary. I looked again at the target area. The first bombers had certainly raised a storm of smoke and debris. The target was a Focke-Wulf airplane assembly plant. Then came "Bombs Away," and I watched the incendiaries tumble out. There seemed to be no end to them. I followed them down and watched thousands of them as they exploded with a flash. The overall effectiveness of the bombing was good, but the bombs of our group apparently fell short of the target. Then we turned due north out over the Bay of Danzig and I noticed that Danzig had been bombed also and many ships out in the harbor were burning. A smoke screen was covering part of the city and also on the easternmost side of the bay.

FIG. 3.5. THE FOCKE-WULF PLANT AT MARIENBURG
These bombing results were cited as a classic example of precision bombing.
(Courtesy of USAAF via James Parton)

Lord I was cramped as we then cut west toward home. Thank God! About halfway back over the Baltic Sea we were attacked by twin engine fighters and some Me-109s. Not very many, but they hounded us, picking off a B-17 here and there. Flying as we were in the tail-end position we got more than our share compared to the rest of the formation. One Me-109 came in within 200 feet straight on our tail. I could see him, but I couldn't get my guns up high enough. Galba in the tail was pouring it to him though, and so was Whitey in the top turret and Beans in the waist. Galba used up 400 rounds of ammo on him and I saw his propeller suddenly stop instantaneously, and he puffed black smoke and began a one-way trip straight down. One B-17 straggler from the formation way back had three fighters on him and went down in flames. Three chutes came out and we saw the fighters circling the chutes. We wondered if they were machine-gunning those poor guys. If we knew they were, then no Jerry would live if he were parachuting down. I would shoot him right to hell. But we weren't sure and had to give them the benefit of the doubt.

The fighters hung on and finally left us at the Danish coast. Our fuel was dangerously low by now. I was so cramped I couldn't move a muscle. We still were a long way from the English coast. At about 6:30 P.M., we sighted England and I sighed hoarsely. I tried to get out of my turret but couldn't. Beans lifted me out and I lay on the floor, in agony every time I tried to move even my head. Harry massaged my limbs and Beans lit a cigarette for me. Boy, it tasted good. I lay there and gradually I began to recover slightly. By the time we had landed and taxied back to our hardstand, I was able to stand in a crouching position. I felt as if I would be better off dead. Upon landing we had only 5 or 6 minutes of fuel left. That is what is known as cutting the tape damn short.

After interrogation, I cleaned my guns, because those two .50 caliber guns are my best friends. I take good care of them, even before myself. After that was finished, I went back to the barracks with the crew and without undressing or even smoking a last cigarette, tumbled onto my cot and was asleep before the springs stopped squeaking.

Only 23 missions to go!

Mission No. 3 — Munster, Germany (October 10, 1943)
The Following Account Was Written by Lt. Marshall J. Thixton

I will cover this mission in some detail. As a reference, I'll use Ian Hawkins *The Munster Raid: Bloody Skies Over Germany*, along with my story and those of our crew members. This was my rude awakening to the fact that war is hell, and we were in the middle of it. I decided my job as a "toggledier" (dropping my bombs on the drop or signal of the lead aircraft) was secondary to just trying to stay alive for 25 missions. I was also assured that if I could survive several missions, I would get to use the Norden Bombsight. As would be expected, the experience of a bombardier who had made many missions was all important to the success of any given mission. By now, the only reason I wanted the bombsight back was because the bomber formation was designed so that the lead aircraft was the safest place to fly. We did lose some lead crews, but in comparison to "tail-end Charlie" (the last plane in the low squadron), lead crew losses were minimal. The reason that the German fighters attacked this low group was because they could attack and then get away before our fighters or most bombers' guns could get full firepower on them. However, this did not apply to the Munster raid. They had so many fighters trying to get to the bombers that they attacked from all angles and all formations. This was the mission that the 100th Bomb Group had only one of their bombers return to their base. Remember, on the missions prior to Marienburg, the 100th Bomb Group suffered severe losses, and that was the reason the 95th Bomb Group had to send three planes to the 100th Bomb Group for the Marienburg mission.

During the Munster mission, our flight into the edge of Germany was fairly uneventful. Our group was protected by our USAAF P-47s and RAF Spitfires. The British Spitfires had the shortest operating defense range of fighter escort planes then in use. The Spits would pick us up at the English channel and protect us to just inside of Europe. Then the P-47s would take over and stay with the B-17s and B-24s nearly to the entry into Germany. A little before the P-47s left, I saw what appeared to be a dark cloud in front of our formation. As we approached closer, I could tell it was not a cloud but a swarm of German fighters. As soon as the P-47s turned back to England, the German fighters made their first attack on our formation. At this time, the bombardier had one .50 caliber machine gun in the nose of the B-17. The navigator had one .50 caliber gun located on the right side of the nose. I could swing my gun to each side and straight ahead. The navigator could almost cover straight ahead and about 30 degrees to the right side of the aircraft. The gun sighting system had a large circle close to the front of the gun and a smaller circle along the end of the gun, very similar to the rifle sights used today, only larger. When the smaller circle had the complete fighter in this circle, it was in the range to be fired on, so one lined up on the fighter with the front larger circle, then waited until the smaller circle was fully covered by the fighter, then the fighter was within range. In the excitement and my first time to actually shoot at an incoming fighter, I opened up on the fighter when it filled up the first circle. I fired about 200 rounds off before the fighter came into range! The armament ground crew loaded the guns prior to flight. They folded the long chain of .50 caliber shells alongside the gun in such a manner that the entire chain would slowly unwind as the gun started firing. After I had started firing too soon and had fired 200 rounds, the gun jammed. When this happened there was a lever on the side of the gun that could be pulled and usually the jam could be cleared. While I was working on the gun to try to get it operational, I looked up and the German fighter that had been firing, flew between our plane and the plane flying next to us. He was so close I could clearly see the German pilot. I went back working on my gun. The next thing I knew, I had been blown completely off the gun, though not off my seat. I was dazed for a few moments, but the cold air flowing into our compartment from a hole in the Plexiglas the size of a basketball quickly revived me. I checked myself over and discovered I was not hit. By then it was time to drop our bombs, so I watched the lead aircraft and when I saw his bombs fall, I salvoed my bombs. I then closed our bomb-bay doors and went back to trying to get my gun to fire, as we were still under fighter attack. Fortunately, I was able to resume firing at the German fighters.

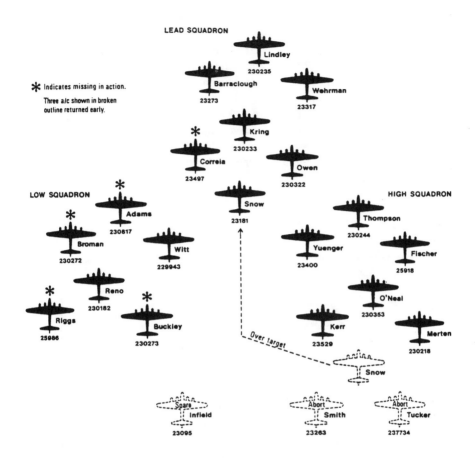

FIG. 3.6. FORMATION OF 95TH BOMB GROUP
FOR MUNSTER MISSION
(Courtesy of Ian Hawkins)

All this happened in approximately 25 minutes. I remember hearing the ball turret gunner, Sgt. George Moffat, on the intercom telling the pilot to pull up. We almost hit a B-17 below us. As the pilot started pulling up, the top turret gunner, Sgt. Donald White, told the pilot to go down, as we were about to hit a plane above us. This could only mean our formation was getting ragged. I guess this was to be expected, since our formation was taking so much fire from fighters and antiaircraft guns. Our crew members were keeping the intercom busy reporting on the aircraft about. B-17s were going down, and some were exploding. Parachutes were floating down almost everywhere. Our parachutes were white, but a few in the sky were of a different color, denoting that some German airmen were paying a price also.

After bombs away, we proceeded to the rally point, where normally we got our formation together. When a plane left the formation, we would try to maintain, as close as we could, our original formation of six "Vs" in our squadron. If possible, any crews in the low squadron would replace those slots in the high squadron or lead squadron. When enemy fighters were attacking it was usually best to delay rather than move around. Shortly after we departed the rally point, the P-47s returned and took on the enemy fighters that were still in the vicinity. You can bet there was never a happier sight than to see our little fighter friends show up.

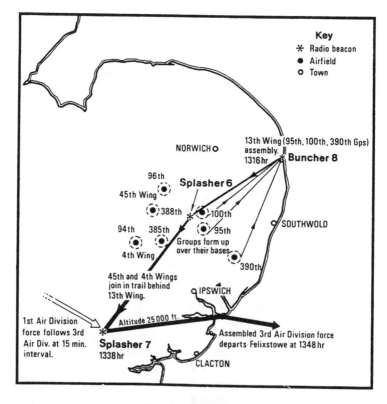

FIG. 3.7. PLAN OF BOMB GROUPS, COMBAT WINGS, AND 1ST AND 3RD AIR
DIVISIONS FOR ASSEMBLY OVER EAST ANGLIA FOR MISSION TO MUNSTER
(Courtesy of Ian Hawkins)

Now to our plane. We had lost two engines and the supercharger was shot out on a third engine, which meant we had only one good engine at high altitude. While the fighters were still attacking, Bill Owen made a very steep dive to lower altitude. No enemy fighters attacked us, most likely because they assumed we were done for. After leveling off around 4,000 feet, one engine returned to full power because it no longer needed the supercharger. To reach altitudes over 20,000 feet, it was necessary to have a supercharger in each engine with the role of forcing more air into the engine. We continued on to lower altitude while still over enemy terrain and fighting to stay in the air. Over the English Channel, the navigator and I moved back to the radio compartment, which was our ditching station. We remained aloft and as we reached the English coast, Bill Owen had all he could do to climb high enough to clear the coastline. Still struggling to keep airborne, we finally reached our base. Never in my life was I so glad to get my feet on the ground. One of the gunners bent down and kissed the good earth. Sgt. Cain, our radio operator, was wounded in the neck. It appeared that a piece of flak entered close to his throat and slid around just underneath his skin. The ambulance came and took Sgt. Cain to the base hospital where the medics removed the flak from the back of his neck. We did not want to even think about the 22 missions we still had to complete. Later, we visited the aircraft we had flown. The ground crew showed us a half-gallon bucket about half full of small chunks of flak they had gathered from our aircraft.

Soon after this mission our crew had a day off, so Bill Owen and I went over to visit the 100th Group's base. Several of our friends from training days had been sent to this base as replacement crews. We did not find many of our friends from training still there, but the ones we did see were very dejected. After the Marienburg mission, there was some discussion of changing the number group designation of the 100th Bomb Group to another number Bomb Group in an effort to rid the 100th of its jinx of suffering heavy losses on bombing missions. However, the crews and personnel of the 100th wanted no part of a change, and the unit remained the 100th Bomb Group. Nearly everyone in the 8th Air Force was convinced that the deadly attacks on the 100th were planned by the German fighter groups, but after the war a German general in charge of fighter operations was invited by the 8th Air Force Historical Society to attend one of their meetings, at which he denied there was any deliberate plan to single the 100th Bomb Group out for repeated attacks. The general stated that when the Luftwaffe attacked a group or formation, the fighters did not have time to identify any one group. The German fighters had their hands full just getting in and out as quickly as possible. The general did say that if they saw a group in a loose formation, they would attack it first. I know our commanders continually tried to keep a tight formation at all times, which was just good operating procedure.

The Following Account of the Mission to Munster, Germany, October 10, 1943, Was Written by S/Sgt. George E. Moffat

It seemed as if we had just closed our eyes when in fact it was five hours later that Jazz came in and tried to wake us for our third raid in as many days. I say tried because he had one devil of a time doing it. The whole operation took well over a half hour. We swore at him, threatened to shoot him on the spot if he didn't let us alone, but Jazz was a very conscientious C.Q., and in the end justice prevailed and we were up. Sometimes I think that is the hardest part of a mission especially as worn out as we were.

We dressed, got our .45 pistols on and scrambled out to the truck. It was cold as charity and black as the ace of spades. We jogged along over the rough road to the mess hall, still growling and half-asleep. The aroma of strong coffee made life seem better though as we went into the mess hall. Fried eggs did wonders too. After the usual discussion at the table about yesterday's raid and wild guesses as to our target for today, we departed for the briefing room. It was 2:30 A.M.

The usual hustle and bustle greeted us in the equipment room as we gathered together our "junk" and checked it over. I found a broken wire in my heated glove and got a new one. Briefing was at 3:15 A.M., and at that time we walked into the map-adorned room and seated ourselves. I'll bet we were a rough-looking bunch with three or four days beard and eyes bloodshot and sunken in. Then Major Jiggs Donohue came in. He looked at us as if to say, "Cheer up boys, the first 25 years are the hardest," and then he pulled back the curtain. The target was Munster, Germany, which is situated on the north side of the Ruhr Valley ("Happy Valley"). We had heard ever since our arrival about "Happy Valley," the flak center of Germany. It was the center of the German industry on the Rhine River.

Major Donohue said there would be about 300 or more Jerry fighters within range and able to attack. As for flak, it would be heavy and accurate. We were so tired that it didn't make a very big impression on us. We merely groaned a little louder. "Jiggs" wished us luck and said, "Today is Sunday. You'll get there just in time to catch them relaxing." "O.K. go out and give 'em hell boys." We went outside into the darkness and loaded our equipment on the truck and rode out to our B-17. She looked big sitting there in the darkness, and beautiful too. The "Liberty Belle" was our baby. And we loved every rivet in her.

I walked over to the armament shack and cleaned my guns and carried them back to the ship. Things were humming now. The mechanics swarmed over her and armorers were fusing the bombs. Our load was 12 high-explosive, 500-pound bombs. A good load. Thank God we weren't carrying those damned incendiaries again. They scare me to death.

Dawn was just cracking when we started engines and waited for the flare signal to taxi out. It came and we waved "so long" to the mechanics as we rolled out of our hardstand and onto the perimeter. Other ships moved out and came in behind and in front of us. We waited again for the signal to take off. Soon, up came the green flare and the B-17s began to roar down the runway. Then our turn came and I felt the ship surge ahead. She seemed to be eager to go, which was more than I was. Our field, dim in the early morning light, fell away behind us and we settled down to Mission No. 3.

We climbed to 24,000 ft. and moved into formation. The 100th Bomb Group was soon sighted and fell in behind us, then the 390th Bomb Group came and moved in ahead and above us. We had 55 planes in our 13th Combat Wing, of the 3rd Air Division. It sure looked good.

FIG. 3.8. THE 95TH BOMB GROUP IN EXCELLENT FORMATION
ON THEIR WAY TO GERMANY
(Courtesy of Boeing Archives via University of Washington Press and Eugene Fletcher)

As we left the English coast, I nodded to Ellsworth Beans and Harry Stotler in the waist, and climbed into my turret and checked my guns, firing them into the channel. The successful test-firing of my guns was always comforting, as it meant to me, I am ready — so far, so good. Before long the enemy coast showed up and so did a P-47 escort. Those 47s looked good and we wished they could stay with us the whole mission. I was tired out, as was everyone on our crew. We pushed inland and met with considerable small areas of flak. Three of the Fortresses turned back because of various problems.

We had 52 planes when we got to the Initial Point (I.P.). The P-47s left us and what happened afterwards, I'll remember if I live to be a thousand years old. No sooner had the escort left than we were hit by about 250 assorted enemy fighters, from Me-109s to Me-210s, and FW-190s. It was even reported that a FW-200 bomber was there. Things got hot as hell. The enemy fighters, many of which were yellow-nosed FW-190s, some of Goering's crack "Abbeville Kids," came at our formation in flights of 15 and 20 from all angles of the clock firing rockets, cannons and machine guns. Some would attack from 12 o'clock and barrel roll right through our formation spitting lead in every direction. I thought as I looked at that swarm, "boy, we bit off more than we can chew this time." The intercom was a constant chatter of voices calling out fighters. As I looked back and down at the 100th Group, I saw ship after ship explode or burn or break up. The sky was full of flak bursts, parachutes, falling wreckage and bodies. I prayed like hell as I threw burst after burst from my guns at diving fighters.

Sergeant Cain called from the radio room and said, "I think I'm the first one to get the Purple Heart, boys." He was hit. We fought on and I saw that the 100th Group was almost gone. All shot down. I couldn't see above us, but I could imagine it was about the same.

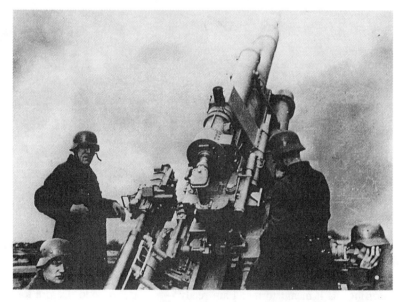

FIG. 3.9. A GERMAN 105 MM FLAK GUN IN ACTION AT MUNSTER
(Courtesy of Ian Hawkins and Wilfried Beer)

The ship on our left suddenly caught fire and in five seconds was a flaming torch. I could see the guys in the waist, guys I slept and ate with, running back and forth trying to get out. A chute popped open too soon and the flames caught it and he went down with no chute. Another jumped and must have forgotten to buckle his leg straps for he slipped through and went plummeting down as his chute flopped lazily behind without a man in it. Then the ship dropped a few hundred feet and blew up.

Our bomb-bay doors came open and I sweated as the "crump" of flak bursting sounded in my ears above the chatter of machine gun fire and engines. Then came "Bombs Away," and I watched them tumble out and sail down. I wanted revenge, and I hoped that the bombs would catch those stinking krauts where it would hurt, anywhere so long as it killed the swine. The bombs made a beautiful pattern right in the heart of the city, and then I began shooting again. The ship on our right, I saw out of the corner of my eye, came swerving toward us out of control and Frank McAllister, our copilot, jockeyed our ship out of the

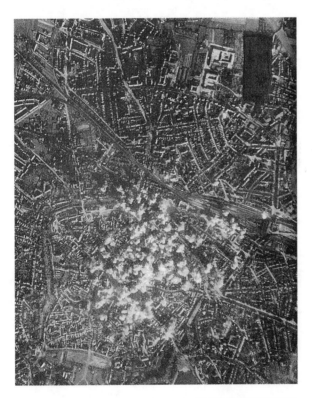

FIG. 3.10. BOMBS LANDING ON TARGET AT MUNSTER
(Courtesy of Ian Hawkins and Leslie Kring)

way as it tore past only inches from colliding with us. As he went down below me I could see he was riddled to pieces. I wondered how many of us were left. I couldn't see *anyone*, but I hoped there were some above us. I also hoped the P-47s would show up. God how I hoped for that. The Jerries continued to attack and flak poured up.

I spotted three Me-210s barreling in at 4 o'clock at about eight hundred yards and got the tail-end boy in my sights. I pressed the trigger button and saw pieces of his tail and fuselage flying off. His tail twisted right off and he went into a spin. A chute popped open.

The other two Me-210s came on in and picking the leader, I fired about 100 rounds at the beggar as he swooped under us and pieces flew off his wing and about three feet of his right wing broke off and he started down. Another chute opened and I was half tempted to shoot the hell out of it, but there were more important things to do. As I was firing at another ship my left gun quit. It was out of ammunition. I continued to fire with my right gun, but after a few

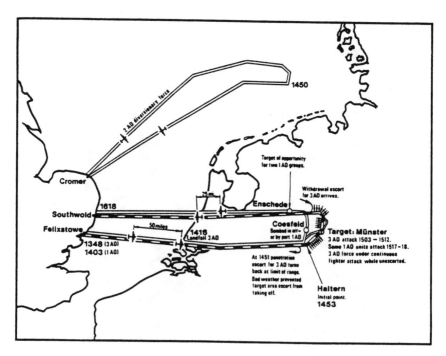

FIG. 3.11. MISSION SUMMARY, MUNSTER, OCT. 10, 1943
(Courtesy of Ian Hawkins)

minutes I could see that the barrel was burned out. At every shot, a 3- or 4-foot belch of flame would shoot out, and the gun was smoking inside my turret. It stopped firing and I assumed that the firing pin must be broken. So I just sat there, sweat rolling down me at 40° below zero, and waved my turret at the attackers. After about five minutes, someone called out that the P-47s were here. The Luftwaffe quit and we saw no more of them. After diving down to about 4,000 feet because we were functioning on one engine, we came back to England on two engines, as the second engine came back to life, as the supercharger was not needed at the lower altitude.

When we were over the North Sea, I got out of my turret and went up to see what had happened to Cain. He was pounding on his radio key, sending out our possible ditching positions. We were not sure if we could make it home or not. The ship was riddled beyond belief. I poured sulfa in the back of Cain's head, and put a cloth in the hole and a bandage over it to stop the blood.

As we were about to land, we fired a red flare, to indicate we had a wounded crew member, and an ambulance came and a crowd gathered as we got Cain out. After the ambulance left, we went to interrogation and chow, then as my guns were worthless, I went to bed. I would have died if I hadn't, I think. The "Liberty Belle" was a wreck and was junked. Out of the 52 planes we started with, 29 were shot down and our wing together destroyed, officially, 102 enemy aircraft.

Only 22 more missions to go!

Mission No. 4 — Schweinfurt, Germany (October 14, 1943)
The Following Account Was Written by Lt. Marshall J. Thixton

If ever there was a mission target that struck fear in the hearts and minds of 8th Air Force bomber crews, it was Schweinfurt! The first combined mission to Schweinfurt/Regensburg made on August 17, 1943 was considered the roughest mission to that time. A total of 60 bombers was lost on that fateful day.

Thus, you can imagine that it was not welcome news to learn our next target was Schweinfurt! We had not fully recovered from the beating we had just received on the Munster mission, and now, we were going to Schweinfurt, which was another 200 miles or so deeper into Germany. The 95th had been scheduled for a mission to Emden, Germany on Oct. 11th, 12th, and 13th, however, two of these missions had been scrubbed, and one was recalled. On a scrubbed mission, you may not have taken off. On a recalled mission, you had taken off, but were called back before entering into Germany. Scrubbed and recalled missions did not count toward your goal of 25 missions. They did have an effect on you, since you had to rise early, be briefed on the mission and then go on standby for several hours. On recalled missions, you did take off and were fully prepared (believe me when I say to get mentally prepared was a struggle) for another mission, only to be called back to base. Poor weather conditions over England and/or Europe were the principal causes of scrubbed and recalled missions.

As I recall, the Schweinfurt mission proceeded into Germany with little or no trouble. After entering Germany, our 3rd Division continued toward Schweinfurt. The 2nd Division (B-24s) was making a diversionary attack to draw German fighters. Then we saw the 1st Division come under heavy attack by hordes of German fighters. The German fighters concentrated on the 1st Division all the way to the target and back, and eventually knocked approximately 60 bombers out of the sky. The 3rd Division was spared the brunt of the fighter attacks, and lost 15 bombers compared to 45 bombers lost by the 1st Division. It was a reversal of the events of the Munster mission, where the 3rd Division bombers had heavy losses and the 1st Division was spared.

The Following Account of the Mission to Schweinfurt, Germany, Oct. 14, 1943, Was Written by S/Sgt. George E. Moffat

After Sunday's raid to Munster, our third in three days, we slept like dead men all day Monday and Monday night. Tuesday morning we got up and fairly ran to the mess hall. We were nearly starved. After practically eating the mess hall out of house and home, we walked happily and contentedly back to the washroom and had a shower and took off nearly a week's stubble of greasy beard, dressed and got a jeep to take us to the 12th Evacuation Hospital where they had taken Sgt. Cain.

As we walked into the hospital, we almost wished we had been hit too. There were pretty nurses all over the place. We found Sgt. Cain in Ward III, but instead of seeing him unconscious and half dead, the beggar was sitting up, his head all bandaged up and giving the prettiest nurse in the ward a big line, gesticulating with his hands and going, "Rat-at-tat-tat-tat." We should have known better than to worry about the varmint. He showed us how, when he drank coffee, it leaked out the back of his fool neck onto the pillow. It did too!

We came back to base in the evening for chow, and I wrote some letters. I hadn't written home for four days and I was afraid they might get worried about me.

We looked on the bulletin board and saw we were on the "Alert" for a mission in the morning, so we hit the hay about 9:00 P.M.

Jazz awakened us about 2 A.M. amid the usual cursing, but not quite so vehemently as last Sunday, and we dressed hastily and left for breakfast. It was awfully cold and the wind was howling, but we were in good spirits. We had enjoyed lots of sleep and food, and a day and night in town. Besides we figured that at the rate we were doing these raids, we would be finished by Christmas and home by Easter. That sure sounded good. So let them send us on every raid that the group made, we didn't care. I felt particularly good, because I found out that I had received official credit for shooting down those two Me-210s on the Munster raid.

After our usual special combat breakfast of fresh eggs, bacon, toast and strong coffee, we left for the briefing room and sat there smoking and laying bets as to our target for today. About 3:30 A.M., Major "Jiggs" came in. He uncovered the map and, as usual, everyone groaned. It was Schweinfurt which was a long haul deep into Germany, and a target that cost the 8th Air Force 60 bombers on the combined Schweinfurt/Regensburg raid in August 1943. We were to hit an extremely vital ball bearing plant and destroy it at all costs. We were to be the second combat wing over the target. The first one getting there about 15 minutes before us. Fighters would be heavy, and flak would be intense and accurate over the target. We were briefed on flak areas enroute to and from the target, and it would be about 48 degrees below zero at our altitude of 26,000 feet.

After cleaning and checking my new set of guns, we went out to our new Liberty Belle II. She was a beauty and I found that the mechanics had painted two swastikas on my turret door. I didn't know whether to bawl them out or kiss them.

After working up a good sweat putting my guns in, I sat down on the grass beside the hardstand and opened a thermos jug of bean soup the Red Cross girls had brought out and smoked a cigarette. It sure was nice to have those pretty Red Cross girls on our side. We talked softly about the raid so that the mechanics couldn't overhear us. When it was time to start engines, we climbed into the ship and taxied on out. I sat in the radio room and then got a bright idea. I took a black pencil and went to the bomb bay. There were 12-500 lb high-explosive bombs on the racks. I scratched on the topmost one, "To Adolf Mit Luff," and signed it, "Owen's Angels." The ship surged ahead and we were off again on mission No. 4, with our fingers crossed, all but our thumb which was on our nose. We had a new radioman in place of Sgt. Cain, a short burly kid with a big smile. He was killed a week later. I don't remember his name.

We gained our full altitude over England and picked up the rest of the wing. As we crossed the English coast, I got in my turret and checked it over and test-fired my guns into the channel. Then I watched the water far below for any convoys to report their position to Bill Owen and Al Engelhardt, our navigator. We saw a few bursts of flak as we crossed the Dutch coast. Al Engelhardt said it must be from Brussels, but it was too inaccurate to worry about.

As we flew on and into Germany, I watched the ground far below. I saw trucks like pinpoints creeping along roads that looked like hairlines. The country looked beautiful, all farmlands and low hills. And I thought I'll bet it's warm down there too, which is more than it is in this ball of ice I'm in. My eyelashes were covered in fine frost, and I broke away the ice in chunks from the exhaust valves of my oxygen mask.

We flew on for hours. I was getting stiff and my eyes were tired from straining to find enemy planes. About 100 miles from Frankfurt, we made an 80 degree diversion south to allow the 1st Division to get ahead of us to the target. When we were 40 miles from Ludwigshaven we turned left once more on course for Schweinfurt. At a little after 12:00 noon we hit our Initial Point and the bomb-bay doors came open. I saw ahead of us about 30 or 40 miles a terrific dogfight over the city. That would be the 1st Division. The flak looked heavy as hell. Someone called out fighters at 3 o'clock high and we were on our toes. I saw some more FW-190s at 12 o'clock low and called them in on the intercom. We bore on toward Schweinfurt. The fighters stabbed in at us and Whitey (Sgt. White) began firing in the upper turret. One was diving on us and Whitey called me as he fired and said, "coming under at 10 o'clock." I swung around and waited. He swooped down and I followed him firing both guns. Whitey and I had a good bit of teamwork operating. The ones at 12 o'clock low

FIG. 3.12. A CLASSIC "BOMBS AWAY"
The "B" on the square background on the tail was the marking
of the 95th Bomb Group.
(Courtesy of USAAF via University of Washington Press and
Eugene Fletcher)

made an attack coming up on their noses from under and I blazed away at them.
There were four FW-190s. I called Whitey as I fired and said, "up and over at
5 o'clock Whitey," and soon I heard his guns chime in with mine. Sgt. Galba
in the tail got in a good burst also. Then Lt. Thixton hollered, "Bombs Away,"
and I followed them down. They landed to the right of the already devastated
city, and hit in a group of factory buildings by the river. Good bombing. I told
Al Engelhardt the results as best I could, and then back we went to chase off
those stinking krauts. The flak was thick now and a few Jerries were around in
their own flak. They were waiting for us to come out. As we came out of the
flak, they hit us again. We had lost quite a few ships already to the flak and the
fighters, and we began losing more.

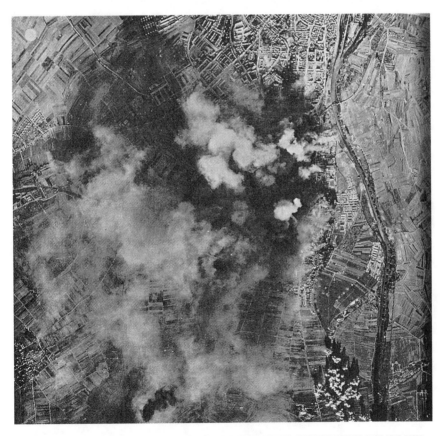

FIG. 3.13. A RECONNAISSANCE PHOTO TAKEN AFTER INCENDIARY BOMBS HIT
THE BALL-BEARING WORKS AT SCHWEINFURT, OCT. 14, 1943
(Courtesy of USAAF via Edward Jablonski)

A ship below us went down a 1,000 feet or so in a dive, and then I saw an amazing thing. He started up again, did a complete loop, leveled out and exploded leaving only a large puff of black, oily smoke. The Jerries continued to attack in groups of threes or fours and fired rockets. Picking us off one by one. I guess a slug came in the wrong place for I suddenly found out to my annoyance that I could talk over the intercom, but I couldn't hear them call out any fighters. I had to watch on my own, and also for guns on other ships firing. Then I spun my turret around to see what they were firing at. Whitey got a Me-109 about this time, though I didn't know about it till we got back because I couldn't hear anything on the intercom.

I was pouring all hell into a twin-engine fighter that was lobbing rockets when my left gun jammed. The ammunition was caught on the baffle plates. I would have to get out of my turret to do anything about it, and as things were too hot, I stayed put and hoped to God the other one didn't screw up on me. I cracked off some more ice from my oxygen mask and cursed the lousy war, and wished I was a chaplain's assistant or something.

The fighters stayed with us for about two hours and knocked off a lot of us. One Fort lagged behind on two engines and was shot down in flames. Two chutes came out. They took one Jerry fighter with them though.

We finally reached the English Channel, and I breathed a deep sigh of relief, even though we weren't quite home. At the English coast, I admired the white cliffs, threw them a hearty kiss and crawled stiffly out of my turret. That first cigarette was worth 100 times its weight in gold.

On landing, we heard that we had lost 60 Forts. Our 3rd Air Division was fortunate in that most of the lost B-17s were from the 1st Air Division. I thought they even underestimated it. Well, the job was done. At any cost! There would be 600 empty chairs tonight for chow at 8th Air Force bomber bases. Mine is going to be full though, thank the Lord. And in a hurry too!

Only 21 missions to go!

CHAPTER 4

AIR COMBAT: FINAL MISSIONS WITH THE
95TH BOMB GROUP (H)
WILHELMSHAVEN — GELSENKIRCHEN

MARSHALL J. THIXTON
GEORGE E. MOFFAT

Mission No. 5 — Duren, Germany (October 20, 1943) Aborted Because of Insufficient Oxygen

The mission to Duren was the only one that our crew aborted or were forced to turn back and head for home. All of us, especially Bill Owen, felt very bad about the reason for our turning back, and also because we were needed on what turned out to be a tough mission. As Sgt. Cain was still grounded from his flak wound, we were furnished a replacement radio operator, whom none of us knew.

After takeoff and assembling with the 390th and 100th Bomb Groups, we noticed our oxygen supply had dropped in uneven spurts. Our flight engineer, Don White, checked all the valves of the oxygen system and found they were okay. As our formation increased its altitude, the oxygen drops continued. Bill Owen knew none of our crew would purposely tamper with the critically necessary oxygen supply, but he also knew it was being done purposely. Bill came on the intercom and in an angry tone said, "we are going to the target with or without oxygen." We were then at about 18,000 feet altitude and Bill ordered all of the crew off oxygen, even though regulations called for air crews to be on oxygen at altitudes above 10,000 feet. We were also below the climbing formation and were, in effect, a straggler B-17, which made us a prime target if any enemy fighters happened by.

As we reached the enemy coast, we were hopelessly below and at a distance from our 13th Combat Wing formation. As our oxygen situation had deteriorated beyond recovery, Bill decided to descend to 10,000 feet altitude and return to base.

When a bomber crew aborted a combat mission over enemy territory the procedure called for a bomb drop on a target of opportunity. In our case, we were not over enemy territory, so the bombs were to be dropped in the Channel or North Sea, as it was considered too risky to carry bombs back to England and land. We dutifully dropped our bomb load in the drink.

No sooner had we landed at Horham, than Major Grif Mumford was waiting for us when we arrived at our hardstand.

Bill told Major Mumford what happened, and Major Mumford had almost already guessed the problem and the cause. Our replacement radio operator had been involved in similar situations before, and had purposely sabotaged our oxygen supply to avoid going into combat.

We were not blamed for aborting, but really wondered why this radio operator was allowed to be on flight crew status, and why we were not warned of what might happen with that maladjusted radio operator.

Mission No. 5 — Wilhelmshaven, Germany (November 3, 1943) The Following Account Was Written by Lt. Marshall J. Thixton

This mission was a "milk run" as our airplane received no flak damage, and we were not attacked by fighters. Two B-17s of our group were damaged which most likely was caused by flak. A milk run was an easy mission which for the majority of the air crews generally meant no attacks by enemy fighters and light to moderate flak over the target. Milk runs were always relative though, as there were seven bombers lost on the Wilhelmshaven mission according to the *Mighty Eighth War Diary* by Roger A. Freeman.

The mission was noteworthy because it was the first time that an Eighth Air Force Pathfinder bomber used H_2X radar which was a U.S. modification of the original RAF H_2S radar. This mission was led by Major Fred Rabo, Commanding Officer of the 812th Bomb Squadron, 482nd Bomb Group, who with other pilots brought the first 12 B-17s equipped with hand-built H_2X radar to England in September 1943. We will get into much more discussion on pathfinders and radar in later chapters.

After we landed, I was taking the adapter off my .50 caliber machine gun, so it could be cleaned, and it slipped out of my hands and struck me in the face. It felt like a mule had kicked me. The adapter was on strong springs to make it easier to swing the gun around when firing at fighters. I had broken a tooth, bloodied my nose and battered my lips. I was slow getting out of the plane and Bill Owen and the rest of the crew had already left for interrogation that followed each mission. I reported to the flight surgeon, and he patched up my face and grounded me for a couple of days. When Bill saw me, he gave me that look that said, "you would do anything to miss a mission." He did have a slight grin, so I guess he wasn't too upset with me. Jokingly, I also asked Bill to see if he could get me a Purple Heart, which was awarded to those wounded in action. I missed the next mission (number 6) to Gelsenkirchen and this meant I was two missions behind Bill.

As our crew was not scheduled to fly again for awhile, I volunteered to fly a make-up mission with another crew. The date was November 11, 1943 and the target was Munster. On this mission, Major Bill Lindley was our pilot and led our Group formation. The eighteen or so B-17s took off at 30-second intervals and started merging into a combat formation. While the group was forming, I went to the bomb bay to pull the safety pins, which allowed the bombs to become "hot." When "hot" bombs were salvoed from the bomb bay, a small fan on the bomb would spin off from the force of the airstream, thus arming the bomb. The pins were a safeguard to keep the fan from accidentally spinning.

Soon after the Group was in proper formation, the mission was recalled because of poor weather. I returned to the bomb bay and started putting the pins back into the arming devices. Apparently Major Lindley was in a hurry to land, as I felt the plane turn on its side in a fighter-type turn, which pinned me to the side of the bomb-bay. Before I could finish reinstalling the pins, we were on our final landing approach, and I hurriedly returned to the nose so I could buckle up for the landing. As I passed the cockpit, I handed the pins I had left to the copilot and told him to have Major Lindley put the pins in the bombs after we landed. There was no great danger unless something went wrong, but things sometimes did go wrong on landings. I guess this type of flying was how the Major got his nickname of "Wild Bill Lindley."

After this experience, I decided not to volunteer to fly missions with other crews. Some of the original crews with the 95th were completing their 25 missions and some of the pilots were flying an extra mission or two so the entire crew could finish together. I was hoping Bill might do this for our crew when we got near the 25-mission goal, but I thought it best not to mention this to Bill until later.

The Following Account of the Mission to Wilhelmshaven, Germany, November 3, 1943, Was Written by S/Sgt. George E. Moffat

Since our aborted mission to Duren and a few scrubbed and recalled missions, we did have a two-day pass and visited London for a few days of rest and relaxation in the big city. For my part I stuck steadfastly to the women and song, taking time out only to carry back to the hotel any members of my crew who had overindulged themselves to the extent that walking seemed extremely hazardous. We all had a good time, each in his own way. At least I came back contented. Even a bit weary!

The evening before the Wilhelmshaven mission, on finding ourselves finally on the alert we almost rejoiced. We had been off alert for so long that we were eager to fight again. We cleaned our Colt .45s and stole some bacon from the mess, and had a good meal before going to bed.

At 2:30 A.M. Jazz came in and awakened us, and was threatened good-naturedly with a waving Colt .45. But, good-naturedly or not, Jazz had no sense of humor when it came to guns, and he hightailed it out as fast as his rickety legs would work. We "haw-hawed" after him and bounced out of bed. I took a long drink of water and lit a cigarette, smiling at Beans, who was gazing at me through sleepy eyes. He wasn't very eager to go. Never was. "For some reason he detested people shooting at him," he said, especially with live ammunition. He continued, "someone is going to get hurt horsing around like that." After the Munster raid, Beans climbed out of the plane, kissed the ground and stared at the ship with her countless ragged holes, then he turned around said, "Well, I'll be goddamned, I just realized something. Do you know that those lousy krauts are using live ammunition on us"? Beans is the "character" of our crew. He's lop-sided with a heart of gold and eats live cigarettes for a whiskey chaser. He has more alcohol in him than blood, and although he's ugly as hell, he's made a lot of women happy.

Getting back to my story, we left for chow and then for the briefing room where Major Jiggs Donohue was already waiting. We seated ourselves and soon he drew aside the curtain on the maps. The boys howled with glee. It was Wilhelmshaven. Right on the north coast and considered a "milk run." I sort of hoped it was as I'd like to see what a milk run was like. We were briefed on the flak which was supposed to be light and fighters which were also to be light. There was a forecast of 10/10 clouds over the target and so we were going to have a pathfinder B-17 leading us.

After briefing we left for our B-17, really in high spirits. We sang as we cleaned our guns and left for the Liberty Belle II. I put my guns in the ball turret and had that secure feeling that all was well. Climbing into the ship the guys asked what I had in my hand, so I showed them Willie. They groaned and began chasing me around the radio room. I laughed myself silly, but I'll be damned if I'd go on a mission without "Willie." He's a wooden soldier about four inches high, and if put on a slated board he'll walk down by himself. He has a big grin on his face even if he is charred and burned in the back from that AT-6 crash in Las Vegas. He hangs by a wire from my guns.

As we waited for the signal for takeoff, I thought about my crew. They were one swell gang. I would fly anywhere with them. They're the best the Air Force has and I'm proud to be one of them. Bill Owen is the pilot, a quiet, unassuming fellow who would give you the shirt off his back. It's our boast that he's never bawled us out. He's so swell that we don't do anything too wrong, because we don't want to disappoint him. I'd fly clear to hell with him and figure I had a good chance of getting back. He is the best pilot I ever flew with and a swell guy to boot.

Frank McAllister (Mac) is the copilot. We kid him about coming from Omak, up in the woods of Washington State. The women follow him around and he loves it. He drinks like a fish and the more he drinks the funnier he gets. He is a nice guy and a natural pilot. Thinks like lightning. Bill and Mac make a perfect combination at those controls.

Al Engelhardt is our navigator. Another number one guy with a heart made of 22 carat gold. And the best navigator the schools have turned out, as you will see in later chapters. He's tall, with dark curly hair and a handsome cuss. He is always neat looking.

Marshall Thixton (Little Bit) is our bombardier and another character. A whole book could be written about him and his exploits. He's small and wiry with a high squeaky Texas drawl. Another swell guy though, and we all love him. He's been trying for months to use his bombsight and in all our missions, he has used it only once, and then he hit the target right smack on the nose, which came as a surprise to all of us, as he had about the worst bombing record in the outfit back in the states.

Don White is our engineer. He is a tall and lanky New Englander who knows his stuff. Never have seen him drunk exactly, but he does drink and appreciates the company of a pretty girl. He is a good egg too.

Lloyd Cain, who was at this time still in the hospital flirting with the nurses, doesn't care much about anything. A sadist I think. He was a hobo before the war and proud of it. He's the most slovenly thing in the world around the barracks, but when there is a 48-hour pass, you never saw a sharper looking article. He does all right with the gals, as he flashes a smile with a Hollywood set of teeth. When the chips are down, he can hold his own with any radio operator.

Harry Stotler is one of our waist gunners. He's the oldest member of the crew at 32. Harry is a rotund, good-natured guy. Weighs about 230 pounds and has a newborn baby back home. Strictly a family man and welcome company. He fires a mean .50 caliber and is a determined fighter. I like him very, very much.

I have already described Ellsworth Beans. To do it again would be a hardship on both you and myself. He is our left waist gunner.

Our tail gunner, Bill Galba, I find hard to write about as he was killed on a mission just two missions after this one. He was quiet, never went out with girls, although he would take a drink. In a sense, he was the brains of the crew. There wasn't a subject he couldn't discuss and chemistry was his favorite. Smart as a whip. He and I were the best friends imaginable. I cried when he died and I'm not ashamed of it. The hardest letter I ever wrote was to his home and his fiancee, Loretta, whom I knew. We used to go on double dates in St. Louis. I still go to the cemetery about once a month with flowers for Bill.

To get back to my story. We took off just about dawn and climbed to our altitude, picked up our formations and headed out over the North Sea. It was bitter cold, but we were happy in a way that we expected this to be a milk run. As it turned out, it was. We turned south over the North Sea and bore down on Wilhelmshaven which was covered with 10/10 clouds. The bomb-bay doors swung open slowly, and a few bursts of flak came up, but low and behind. The pathfinder ship had a problem somehow, and we made a 360 degree turn over the target and dropped on his smoke bombs on the second bomb run. I was thankful the flak was not heavy. I'd hate to have to go over Bremen twice. The bombs sailed away and I watched them until they disappeared through the clouds and then swung back up looking in vain for any enemy fighters. This was truly a milk run.

We turned west and headed back toward England, slowly letting down. As we crossed the English coast, I emerged from my turret and lit a cigarette. We all smiled at this mission and prayed like hell that the remaining 20 would be the same. We landed, taxied up to our hardstand and were met by Red Cross girls with coffee and cake. Not bad looking, the girls, I mean. It's not such a bad war after all we decided. Especially with plans of going into town that night if we weren't on the alert.

Only 20 missions to go!

Mission No. 6 — Gelsenkirchen, Germany (November 5, 1943)

Due to the injuries I received when my .50 caliber slipped and struck me in the face after returning from Wilhelmshaven, I was still grounded and missed the mission to Gelsenkirchen. Fortunately, George Moffat did his usual fine job of recording the details of this mission and his story follows.

The Following Account of the Mission to Gelsenkirchen, Germany, November 5, 1943, Was Written by S/Sgt. George E. Moffat

After our raid on Wilhelmshaven, our faith was considerably restored. We had actually been on a "milk run" and were in high spirits. We went back to the barracks and found we were not alerted for the next day so we washed up, wrote some letters, and then hit the sack. The next morning when we awakened about 9:00 A.M. we dressed up in our class A uniforms (olive drab trousers and blouse and overseas cap) and headed for town. After a very enjoyable day we contemplated staying overnight, so we called the squadron by phone and asked if there was a "baseball game" on tomorrow. There was. It was a good thing we called. Coming back it was a long 20 miles and it was late. We had to be back by 1:30 or 2:00 A.M. at the latest. Rides were few and far between and Beans and Whitey were tanked, which certainly didn't help us any. We arrived home, by the love of God, at 1:45 A.M., just as Jazz was making his rounds to wake everyone for the day's mission.

We dressed in our flying clothes and headed for the mess hall after soaking Beans and Whitey under the cold shower. It did wonders and with the amount of walking we had done, they were pretty well sober. We decided that we had better be more careful in the future and leave plenty of time to get home, for if we failed to show up for a mission, we would really be in the soup. The way the raids were adding up for us, we figured, God willing, we'd be finished with our 25 missions, and home by Easter at the latest.

After the usual morning confab on what our target might be, we got back to the trucks and went out to the equipment room, where I beat the supply man out of a new pair of heated gloves, checked over my junk and sat down in the briefing room smoking a cigarette and staring at the veiled map on the wall, wondering.

After about 15 minutes the room was packed and Major Jiggs came in. I could tell by his face that it was not going to be a milk run. He really took his "boys" welfare to heart. When he unveiled the target map, there were varied remarks, none of which I can record here. It was a target we had hoped we would never see and one which everyone talked about. It was "Happy Valley" in the Ruhr. Also called "Flak Valley" because of the intense flak encountered. There were many wild tales about that place and we were soon to see for ourselves that although the tales were wild, they were also true.

The course we were to take seemed very foolish to me. We were to attack from the north, then after hitting our target were to turn 90 degrees right on a heading of 270 degrees which would take us directly down the whole length of the lousy Ruhr Valley. We swore at the dope who had charted our course over every possible flak area, but had to be content with the theory, "ours not to wonder why, but only to do or die." By the way, being not in the least optimistic, we fully expected to do the latter. We were briefed to fly at 27,100 feet. Target was to be clear of clouds and the temperature would be 53 degrees below zero at altitude. Take-off was at 6:13 A.M.

We left the briefing room and loaded our equipment on the trucks, then took off for our ship. Liberty Belle II was on the same hardstand as our old baby. She was a brand new crate: a "G" model with a chin turret and we were happy as a bunch of kids with a new toy. The B-17G also had gun mounts through closed waist windows, which was a real improvement over the open waist windows of the B-17F. After dumping our stuff we headed for the gun shack where we cleaned and oiled up our "best friends" and carried them back to install them. The morning was dark as the inside of a cat and cold as charity. The wind was blowing gusts of snow and sleet and I shivered, partly with the cold and partly with the excitement of the coming battle. Beans slouched along a pace or so behind mumbling something about not coming back from this party. He always was a cheerful cuss. God bless him.

I put my guns in, my fingers were so cold I could barely hold a screwdriver, and was constantly scraping the skin off my knuckles. I cursed the day I had joined the Army. Finally, I finished and up rolled a jeep with thermos bottles full of hot soup. Bean soup. It was always bean soup. I still can't look a bean in the face. Everyone finished about the same time and we sat smoking. The lights came on in the house in back of our hardstand. The tail of the Liberty

Belle II was nearly in her backyard. They arose very early in the morning, and were usually out to see us off and also there again on our return, with a cup of tea and cakes. Her name was Mrs. McRoberts.

Finally, the time came to start engines and we all crawled in the ship. Soon we taxied out and got in line for the takeoff. At 6:30 A.M., we gathered speed down the runway. It seemed an eternity before we finally lifted off the ground with that load of 500-pound bombs. I think I sweat the takeoffs as much as I do being over the target.

We climbed to 18,000 feet where the group formed and headed for the assembly point over splasher number 6. I sat in the radio room dozing, plugged into a walk-around oxygen container, until we passed over the English coast, then climbed down into my turret and checked my guns and equipment over. The wind was whistling through the cracks of the door at my back, and at 18,000 ft. the frost was on my eyelashes and I was shivering even under the hot-suit. We sighted the enemy coast and went in just south of Amsterdam. That belligerent city annoyed us a little with a few well-placed bursts of flak, but did no harm. We passed over Holland and into Germany.

No one had to tell me we were nearing our I.P. (Initial Point). I saw it from 75 miles away. I had never before seen such an antiaircraft barrage. As far as the eye could see in every direction there were black clumps of bursting flak. They must have been shooting at the first bunch over. We were the second wave. As we came closer, we encountered numerous enemy fighters, but the majority of them were attacking the low groups. We were at 27,500 feet and I could see some of the German fighters attempt to reach us, but they couldn't quite get that high. They would swoop up and then fall off a few thousand feet below. Some of the Abbeville Kids with their yellow-nosed Focke-Wulf fighters were there. I cut loose at a few who managed to coax their crates up near us, but I couldn't see that my bullets did much damage.

A B-17 directly below us suddenly heaved upwards in its center and fell off in two sections. No chutes emerged. Then we were in the flak. I've never seen flak so thick before. It made a thumping noise and threw us around wildly. A number of our ships exploded below and in back of us, a Focke-Wulf fighter miscalculated his dive and crashed through a Fortress on my left. The whole bomb load and the two ships exploded in a puff of smoke and flames. The blast nearly careened us into the ship next to us. I could hear the ping and whistle of flak hitting us, and I tried vainly to make myself smaller. I watched as our bomb-bay doors opened and then "bombs away" came and our load sailed down through the flak. They landed on and closely around our target.

We fought off fighters and waded through that lousy flak for 21 minutes coming west along the Ruhr Valley, and I swore and cursed the lamebrain who had planned this route back to England for us. The flak picked off a good number of us, but it finally ended as we came out of the valley and the sweat on my face now froze. We had an engine out and I was mad. The lousy krauts had made plenty of holes in our nice new airplane. We landed, and off we went to interrogation, to eat and then to the sack.

Only 19 missions to go!

TRANSFER TO 482ND BOMB GROUP (PATHFINDER) AT ALCONBURY

The mission to Gelsenkirchen, Germany on November 5, 1943 was the final mission we as a complete crew would fly as members of the 95th Bomb Group. On November 14, 1943, our crew was informed we were being transferred to the 482nd Bomb Group (Pathfinder) at Alconbury.

In our short tour of duty at the 95th Bomb Group, we as a crew had flown six missions and Bill Owen had flown seven missions. Our crew flew all four missions of Black Week which not too many crews did and survived. From our first mission on October 8, 1943 until we left on November 14, 1943, the 95th flew only two missions that we were not scheduled to fly. We were all sorry to leave the 95th.

CHAPTER 5

THE 482ND BOMB GROUP (P)
AN OVERVIEW

JOHN J. O'NEIL

This Chapter Was Written by John O'Neil, Who in December, 1943 Joined Lt. Owen's Crew as a Replacement Tail Gunner/Waist Gunner

The 482nd Bomb Group (P) was activated on August 20, 1943 at USAAF Station 102, Alconbury, Huntingdonshire, England. The "P" stood for Pathfinder and meant the 482nd would lead the Eighth Air Force on combat missions over Europe by means of radar and other electronic navigational devices. The 482nd has the distinction of being the only USAAF group to be activated outside of the United States. For some time it was obvious that because of bad weather over Europe, especially during the winters, the Eighth Air Force

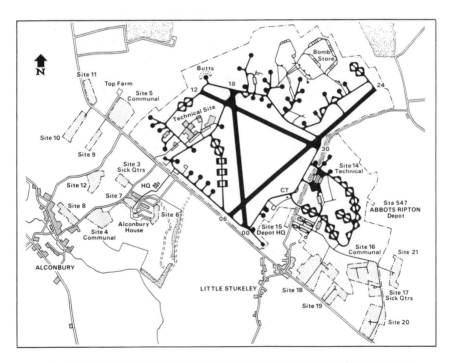

FIG. 5.1. DIAGRAM OF USAAF 482ND BOMB GROUP BASE AT ALCONBURY
The 813th Bomb Squadron Headquarters was in the Site 6 area (left center, lower portion).
(Courtesy of USAAF via Pat Carty)

needed a radar capability to bomb Germany during periods of partial or complete cloud cover. During the winter months, there were only two or three days each month of clear weather over Europe, which would allow navigation by dead reckoning and use of the Norden bombsight. Fortunately for the Eighth, British scientists had developed a radar system at the University of Birmingham about 1940, which was used by the RAF on bombing missions and would be available for use by the Eighth. Lt. Colonel William S. Cowart, Jr. was a key man in the organization of the 482nd Bomb Group, and is credited with the modification and installation of RAF radar, H_2S or "Stinky" model, in B-17s and B-24s.

FIG. 5.2. A B-17 AT ALCONBURY EQUIPPED WITH H_2S (STINKY) RADAR
The radar dome is mounted under the nose of the airplane and
was called a "bathtub" by airmen.
(Courtesy of USAAF via Roger A. Freeman)

FIG. 5.3. A B-17 ON A PRACTICE MISSION WITH ITS H_2S
RADOME UNDER THE NOSE
(Courtesy of USAAF via Roger A. Freeman)

When England was fighting alone before Pearl Harbor, a prototype radar unit was sent to the United States under an agreement whereby U.S. industrial capability would undertake the development of radar. The British thinking also was that if England was invaded by the Germans it would be preferable for security reasons for radar research and development to be going on in the U.S. In November 1940, the Radiation Laboratory was established at the Massachusetts Institute of Technology, and the American version of radar named Mickey (H_2X) was eventually developed, hand-built, installed in twelve B-17s and flown under the command of Major Fred Rabo in September 1943 to Alconbury for use by the 482nd.

FIG. 5.4. ONE OF THE TWELVE B-17S WITH H_2X (MICKEY) RADAR
THAT WERE "HAND-BUILT"
The radar dome was mounted to the rear of the chin turret guns. Later factory-built H_2X radar
equipped B-17s had the radome mounted in the ball turret position.
(Courtesy of USAAF via Roger A. Freeman)

Of the radar systems, H_2S, H_2X and later Eagle, H_2X was the main system used by the 8th Air Force. These radar systems were basically pilotage and target-finding units by which a beam of transmitted energy scanned the ground areas. The reflected signals gave a maplike picture on the unit screen in the bomber, with dark areas for water, light areas for ground, and bright areas for towns and cities. The actual navigation was done by a comparison of the radar picture with a map.

The 482nd Bomb Group originally consisted of the 812th, 813th and 814th Bomb Squadrons. The 812th and 813th flew B-17s and the 814th flew B-24s. Later on in February 1945, the 36th Bomb Squadron RCM joined the 482nd and remained at Alconbury till the European war ended in May 1945. The RCM designation for the 36th stood for radio countermeasures, which meant the 36th flew missions with special electronic equipment designed to jam the radar and other electronic equipment of the German Air Force and antiaircraft batteries. Interestingly, the 36th flew B-17s, B-24s and also P-38 fighters.

In addition to the bomb squadrons of the 482nd, supporting personnel at Alconbury comprised the 329th Service Squadron, 41st Station Complement Squadron, 1251st Military Police Co., 861st Chemical Company, and the 1114th Quartermaster Company.

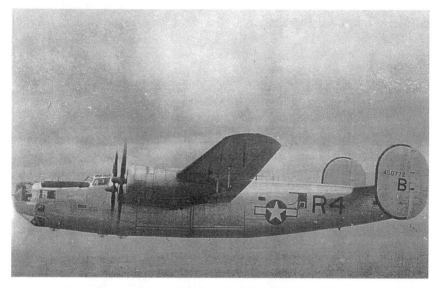

FIG. 5.5. A RCM B-24 OF THE 36TH BOMB SQUADRON
The B-24 has radio countermeasure equipment including an underwing "Mandrell" and "Dina" antennae, and a "Jostle" antenna on the top of the fuselage.
(Courtesy of USAAF via Pat Carty)

Although the RAF had tried daylight bombing of targets in Europe early in the war, they had for a long time carried out only night bombing missions. When the Eighth first began flying missions in mid-1942 from England to targets in Europe, these raids were all done in daylight. The RAF felt that American losses would be prohibitive on daylight bombing raids, and tried to persuade General Ira Eaker to switch to night missions. General Eaker was convinced that the Eighth could be successful in daylight missions and sold Prime Minister Churchill on the idea of round-the-clock bombing of Europe with the RAF hitting targets at night and the USAAF following up with daylight raids. A major factor in the success of the Eighth Air Force in the winter of 1943-1944 was the contribution of the 482nd Bomb Group in leading 48 day missions and attacking 69 individual targets in Germany.

FIG. 5.6. A B-17 EQUIPPED WITH H₂X (MICKEY) RADAR LEADS FORTRESSES
ON A MISSION TO GERMANY
The H₂X radome was mounted in the ball turret position (mid-lower part of the airplane).
Other B-17s can be seen in formation in the background.
(Courtesy of USAAF via Edward Jablonski and Cecil Cohen)

The 482nd Bomb Group, with a skeleton force, began work at Alconbury
to convert the base into a four-squadron operational group and make the base
ready to receive the incoming planes and crews. The bulk of the personnel came
from the 92nd Bomb Group, the 479th Anti-sub Group, and the 12th
Replacement Depot. Some of the new crews came from the states via Valley Air
Base in Wales. Other crews were furnished by the bomb groups already in
combat and scattered throughout England in the Eighth Air Force. Some 482nd
replacement gunners were recruited from various U.S. Army units in England
and trained as aerial gunners at RAF/USAAF bases in England. A feverish
activity went on at the 482nd for 36 days. Then on the night of September 26,
1943, four H₂S radar-equipped B-17s of the 482nd were flown to bases of the
1st and 3rd Air Divisions to prepare to lead the mission of the next day. The
four pathfinder crews were alerted and in the evening loaded all equipment,
including bombs, into their B-17s and took off and flew in blacked-out England
to designated Eighth bomber bases. The pathfinder crews were bedded down for
a few hours and got an early-morning call to go to briefing with the rest of the
air crews. The target of this mission was Emden, Germany.

Of the two pathfinder B-17s sent to the 1st Division, one of these B-17s
piloted by Maj. Clement Bird, Commanding Officer of the 813th Bomb Sq., had
operational problems with the radar equipment and turned the lead position over

to the second radar B-17 piloted by Lt. K.W. Gurney. Faulty radar equipment prevented one of the pathfinder ships sent to the 3rd Division from taking off. However, the backup pathfinder B-17 did lead the 3rd Division bombers. The attacking B-17s dropped their bombs on the pathfinder's marker flares, and some bombs hit the docks at Emden but most fell around the city. The mission was judged successful because pilotage points were picked up which indicated the bomber formations had passed over the target with the help of the 482nd Pathfinders.

About 30 to 40 Me-109s fighters attacked the lead aircraft in pairs and fours using the sun and vapor trails to good advantage. No losses or injuries were sustained by the 482nd, but 2 of the 3 pathfinder B-17s had minor battle damage. For the mission interrogation, the pathfinder B-17s returned to the bomber bases from which they had taken off. After interrogation, the pathfinders then flew home to Alconbury.

According to the *Mighty Eighth War Diary* (Freeman), a total of 308 B-17s took part in the mission and were escorted by 262 P-47s. There were seven B-17s and one P-47 lost due to enemy action.

It is recorded in official 482nd Bomb Group records that from that date on the Group made history. The Eighth Air Force, instead of being shackled to the ground as in the winter of 1942-1943, flew on under the combat leadership of 482nd crews to set a new combat record. In addition to the 48 day missions led by the 482nd, 16 night missions were flown testing "Oboe" navigational equipment. Oboe was the first of a series of radar beacon bombing devices that the British had developed, and though accurate, was limited to short-range distances. Table 5.1 lists the major German targets of the 482nd. A 482nd B-17 was credited with being the first American bomber over Berlin. This B-17 was piloted by Lt. Bill Owen and the mission will be covered in a separate chapter.

TABLE 5.1
MAJOR TARGETS (IN GERMANY) OF 482ND BG

Target	Number of Missions Flown
Brunswick	7
Bremen	6
Frankfurt	6
Berlin	5
Munster	4
Ludwigshaven	4

The 482nd at Alconbury was visited by the commanding general of the Eighth Air Force, Ira C. Eaker, who came just before the radar-led missions began, to inform the officers and men of the 482nd that the Eighth was depending on the 482nd as the first U.S. pathfinder group to lead bombing missions to Europe during periods of cloud cover. The 482nd was also honored by a visit of King George VI and Queen Elizabeth, which was an impressive event for personnel of the 482nd.

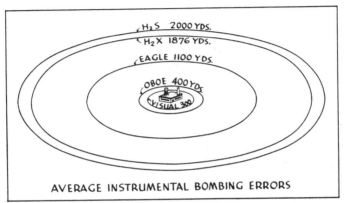

AVERAGE INSTRUMENTAL BOMBING ERRORS

FIG. 5.7. AVERAGE BOMBING ERRORS OF H₂S, H₂X, EAGLE, OBOE AND VISUAL
Oboe, though accurate, was not effective beyond short-range distances.
(Courtesy of American Institute of Physics)

A major concern of the pathfinders at Alconbury was whether German Intelligence would order a bombing strike against the 482nd, which could have destroyed all of the pathfinder equipment of the Eighth, not to mention the aircraft of the 36th Squadron, which was also involved in highly secret work. Also considered was whether the Germans would launch a parachute drop with commandos to destroy the pathfinder airplanes as they sat on the hardstands. Special night guard duty assignments on radar-equipped B-17s and B-24s were carried out by aerial gunners of the 482nd as a precautionary measure. But the Germans did not act and the special guard duty was discontinued, much to the delight of the gunners.

The Eighth also decided to disperse its pathfinder crews and airplanes. The 482nd then began training crews to become pathfinders for assignment in the three air divisions. Thus in February and March of 1944, the 482nd led combat missions, trained crews to be pathfinders, and modified new pathfinder aircraft, which would be sent to dispersed squadrons throughout the Eighth Air Force.

On March 22, 1944, the 482nd led its last daylight bombing mission. Crews of the 482nd did however fly daylight strikes in support of D-Day operations. After March 22nd the main job of the 482nd was to train new navigators who had been previously checked out on "Mickey" radar in the states. Air crew personnel of the 482nd were given the choice of remaining at Alconbury or transferring to other bomber bases to complete their tours of combat missions. The 482nd did fly single-plane missions at night into Germany to do mapping by means of scope pictures, as an aid to other pathfinder groups. These night missions by the 482nd continued up to the end of the war in Europe, and also allowed pathfinders a means of completing their mission tours.

The 36th Bomb Squadron carried out radar countermeasures missions from June 6, 1944 to April 30, 1945. The 36th joined the 482nd on February 27, 1945 and remained at Alconbury until after the war ended, and in fact was the last squadron to leave Alconbury. Individual bomb groups had radio countermeasure equipment, but the 36th was the only squadron designed exclusively as an 8th Air Force RCM squadron (Hutton 1994).

Some of the duties of the 36th included jamming of enemy radar, screening of Eighth bombers' very high frequency (VHF) channels while bombers were assembling, carrying out "spoof" raids, jamming enemy tank communications, and performing special electronic search missions. It is impossible to fully evaluate the number of air crews, as well as bomber and fighter aircraft, saved when enemy fighters discovered too late the essential interception data.

According to Alfred Price in his book: *History of U.S. Electronic Warfare*, "using conservative estimates, radio countermeasures probably saved about 600 Air Force heavy bombers during operations over Europe. In the Pacific, the use of countermeasures probably saved some 200 B-29 Superfortresses."

When the happy day of war's end in Europe came in early May 1945, the 482nd was given a new assignment to relocate to Victorville, California, and continue to train navigators in the intricacies of bombing by radar. Thus, in latter May 1945, B-17s of the 482nd took off from Alconbury for the last time and headed for Valley Air Base in Wales. Each B-17 carried a total of 20 airmen and ground personnel. After an overnight stay at Valley, the next stop was Reykjavik, Iceland. Again, a brief stay and takeoff for Goose Bay, Labrador. After a short rest and refueling, the final destination was Bradley Field, Windsor Locks, Connecticut. After being routed to bases near their homes, all personnel were given 30-day furloughs. And some 482nd people were sent back to the states across the Atlantic by ship. On returning from furloughs, all 482nd airmen and ground personnel were supposed to report to Victorville. As often happened in the Army, something interfered and many 482nd people were detoured before reaching Victorville, and some were slated for discharge from the service even before the war ended in the Pacific in early August. This is a brief overview of the 482nd Bomb Group (P), and now we will discuss in greater detail specific missions and activities of Lt. Owen and his crew in the 482nd.

CHAPTER 6

AIR COMBAT: 482ND BOMB GROUP (P)
SOLINGEN — BREMEN — LUDWIGSHAFEN

MARSHALL J. THIXTON
GEORGE E. MOFFAT
JOHN J. O'NEIL

Our crew reported to the 482nd Bomb Group (P), 813th Bomb Squadron at Alconbury on November 19, 1943. We reported and signed in, and once again our full crew was together. I suspect it was because of two things: we didn't dare foul up again and they drove us over to the 482nd Bomb Group base in an army truck. After reporting, we walked down a road to the enlisted men quarters. Then we four officers proceeded down the road to what we thought would carry us to our barracks area. We came to a split in the road and we continued to a building we could see ahead of us. There were several buildings in the area and we found one that looked like a living area and set up housekeeping, figuring the barracks area must be close by. We learned later that the barracks area was a quarter mile down the other road. Since we were already set up, we decided to stay.

Our enlisted crew members found us and looked around to see what was in the other buildings. In one they found canned goods stored. I thought it was probably mostly Spam and vegetables, but there were several jars of jam. The small town of Alconbury was down the road about another quarter mile and it had a bakery. This bakery operated differently than any we had ever seen, since when the bread was ready to take out of the ovens, it was dumped on the floor. The floor was kept fairly clean, and although the bakers and others walked on the floor, it didn't seem to hurt the steaming hot bread. Our crew soon learned the baking schedules and when bread came out of the ovens, we would pick up several loaves and take them back to our quarters. Butter came from someplace and we would feast on hot buttered bread and jelly. We stayed in this building a little over a month before we were forced to move. I always believed the mess sergeant started missing jelly, and maybe other things, and had us moved. Anyway, by then we had met several of the flight crews and were ready to move into the barracks with them.

Unfortunately, we do not have the records of each flight as were available while flying with the 95th Bomb Group. This is primarily due to two causes: first, and most important, is that since we were bombing under 10/10 (complete) cloud cover, results were not immediately available, and second, since the 482nd crews flew their missions as lead planes for the other bomb groups, we did not have the input that came from regular group interrogations, in which eighteen

71

or more crews participated after returning from a mission. Therefore, bomber losses on the missions, were not known and overall results of bombing missions were lacking or incomplete.

I am listing the missions our crew flew with the 482nd Bomb Group as taken from the records of Lt. Bill Owen.

Mission	1.	Solingen, Germany	Dec.	1, '43
	2.	Bremen, Germany	Dec.	20, '43
	3.	Ludwigshafen, Germany	Dec.	30, '43
	4.	Kiel, Germany	Jan.	4, '44
	5.	Frankfurt, Germany	Feb.	4, '44
	6.	Leipzig, Germany	Feb.	20, '44
	7.	Frankfurt, Germany	Mar.	2, '44
	8.	Berlin, Germany	Mar.	4, '44
	9.	Berlin, Germany	Mar.	9, '44
	10.	Special Mission	Apr.	22, '44
	11.	Special Mission	Apr.	24, '44
	12.	Special Mission	May	27, '44
	13.	France (D-Day)	June	6, '44
	14.	Special Mission	July	19, '44

Also, you may note that our missions were flown with fairly long intervals between flights. This was because pathfinders flew only when cloud cover was forecasted over Germany. Since the prevailing weather would move east from England into Europe, it was seldom that conditions were favorable in England and Germany at the same time. The pathfinder crews would be alerted for a mission, only to be cancelled because of weather conditions. Each squadron of pathfinders, two B-17 squadrons and one B-24 squadron, had at least eighteen crews assigned. During the winter of 1943-1944, the entire 8th Air Force maximum effort was 750 to 1,000 planes available, or approximately 48 groups. The 482nd could not furnish 48 pathfinder aircraft at one time, so each group would not always have a pathfinder aircraft. This is one reason that some bomb groups dropped on flares dropped by the groups led with a pathfinder aircraft. I remember flying over a city we had bombed the day before and I could see where bombs had been dropped up to a mile from the city. The bomb pattern was in a tight cluster, which would not be seen with British night bombing. I remember that we did fly a day mission to Leipzig after the British had bombed it the previous night. There was snow on the ground, and we could see bomb craters from our initial point (I.P.) to the target that were made by RAF bombers the previous night. When we flew over Leipzig, fires were still burning in the city indicating that RAF bombers had indeed clobbered the city in their night raid.

Mission No. 7 — Solingen, Germany (December 1, 1943)

On December 1, 1943, Bill Owen's crew flew its first mission with the 482nd Bomb Group. The target was Solingen. Somehow, I missed this mission. I know that I was very unhappy about the setup for bombardiers at the 482nd. I recalled my statement to Al Engelhardt when he joined the crew and I found out he was qualified as a navigator and bombardier. I had told him that he would do the navigating and I would do the bombing. With the pathfinder bombing procedure, the navigator does the navigating and also tells the bombardier when to drop the bombs. When the pathfinder drops its bombs, all planes in the group drop also. At least I now had a bombsight, but little chance of using it. I suspect that this had something to do with me missing the mission to Solingen.

From the 482nd Bomb Group records, the 482nd dispatched six aircraft to lead B-17s of the 1st Air Division to bomb Leverkusen and Solingen. All combat wings attacked Solingen, because the radar (H_2X) equipment of only one pathfinder was working, and all other combat wings bombed on its sky markers. The pathfinder planes carried two smoke bombs, which were dropped simultaneously with the bombs in the bomb bay, so that the other 17 planes in the group formation could more easily observe the bomb drop. Of course, with complete 10/10 cloud cover, the bombing results could not be determined by the bomber crews, so results were obtained by photo reconnaissance planes.

Continuing from the 482nd Bomb Group history of the mission to Solingen, about 30 German fighters pressed home and persisted with vigorous attacks. Flak was reported as intense, causing battle damage to two pathfinder planes. On this mission we lost our first crew member, S/Sgt. William A. Galba, tail gunner, who died from lack of oxygen on the way back to England.

I was deeply interested, not only because we had lost a crew member and friend, but also because I had not gone on the mission and the copilot, or bombardier, usually requested all crew members to come on intercom and report, "oxygen OK." From what I learned from Bill Owen and other crew members, it appears that no one could have prevented this tragic outcome. I know that Bill Owen was deeply affected by this loss. I remember he worked for a week writing a letter to S/Sgt. Galba's father. He offered to take a picture of S/Sgt. Galba's grave and send it to his father. To my knowledge, Bill never heard from S/Sgt. Galba's father. S/Sgt. John J. O'Neil replaced S/Sgt. Galba as tail gunner.

S/Sgt. George E. Moffat in his story of the Solingen mission provides more details of the untimely death of S/Sgt. William A. Galba.

The Following Account of the Mission to Solingen, Germany, December 1, 1943, Was Written by S/Sgt. George E. Moffat

A good many things happened to us since our raid on Gelsenkerchen. One afternoon, November 14th to be exact, we were told that we were being transferred to become a pathfinder crew. We didn't want to go for we liked the 95th and everyone there. We had a good deal and we knew it. If we left, we didn't know what we were getting into. There were various rumors concerning pathfinders (PF). They were new then. One was that the PF ship went on missions only when it was cloudy and it went on ahead of the rest of the bombers, dropped down below the clouds to spot the target and fired flares up through for the rest to drop on. And also that a pathfinder crew pulled only five missions, but that damn few ever finished because being alone they were always shot down by fighters. All the rumors didn't make it any easier to swallow. But as we found out the rumors proved to be false. It was radar equipment that was used to see through the clouds and we still had 25 missions to complete. Before we left the 95th, the boys, still believing in their rumors, looked at us with that "you're as good as dead" expression on their faces and we thought so too. We made the rounds and said goodbye to everyone and packed our clothes.

On arriving at the 482nd Bomb Group (P), we were told to report to the 813th Squadron, and immediately walked into the orderly room and told First Sgt. Raleigh Lyles we weren't happy with our transfer from the 95th BG to the 482nd BG and we didn't care who knew it. We always felt this exchange put us on his blacklist. We subsequently spent several hectic weeks until we were finally tamed somewhat and became more or less accustomed to our lot, and made peace with Sgt. Lyles.

It was December 1st before we were called to pull a raid. And it was much different from what we were used to. We loaded our guns and equipment on the B-17 about 10 P.M. the night before the raid and then were assigned a group to lead. Then we took off for that group's base.

We were hoping to be sent as the pathfinder to lead our old 95th Bomb Group, but instead were sent to a base in the 1st Bomb Division.

When we landed at this strange, to us, air base about 11 P.M., we were welcomed by some ground crew and MPs who would stand guard on our radar-equipped B-17. A truck finally took us to a barracks and we lay down for a couple of hours till they awakened us at 1:30 A.M.

We got up and being already dressed headed straight for the mess hall to eat our fill of fried eggs, bacon, toast and black coffee.

After that wonderful breakfast, we went to briefing. We really felt like loners among these combat crews, and the briefing officer was not as reassuring as Major Jiggs Donohue. When the map was unveiled, we thought, oh no, it was Solingen, right in the damn Ruhr. Flak Valley, twice in a row. Phooey! We were to fly at 26,000 ft. Flak was to be heavy and accurate and we "could" be attacked by 250 single-engine and 330 twin-engine fighters. Beans left briefing with his chin on the floor as usual and I gave him a friendly boot in the behind as we went out the door.

Back out at the ship, I helped Galba put in his guns after completing my own and we sat down by the tail and smoked a cigarette together, wondering whether to go to the show back at our base or not. Then at 6:13 A.M. we started engines and climbed in. This should be a good scrap we figured.

At 6:41 A.M. we took off carrying eight 500-lb. bombs; assembled the group at 20,000 ft; and then flew to join up with the other groups to complete the wing formation. At 9:03 A.M. we left the English coast and headed for Germany.

We passed the enemy coast without seeing any opposition of any kind and flew on toward Germany with the whole wing behind us. It made us feel good to know we were leading the whole show. There was no flak or fighters until we neared our Initial Point of the bombing run. It was deadly cold as usual and I was rolled up in my ball turret with the wind whistling around me, and my feet and hands aching with the cold.

As we turned north on the I.P. toward our target about 30 or so fighters began horsing about looking us over, and we sat quietly and looked back at them. We always let them start the fight because after all, our main purpose is not to destroy fighters, but to hit that target. The enemy planes did attack and then the flak came pouring up from "Happy Valley." We were in it up to our necks. The fighters were coming in through their own flak barrage to get us and things got plenty hot. Some of the Abbeville Kids were there, and I concentrated on them firing both guns as they barrel-rolled through our formation. One went off in a spin and I lost him through the clouds below, so I didn't bother reporting him. The flak bursting and engines and wind and machine gun fire was deafening even through my helmet. I could hear Galba and the waist gunners pouring it to the fighters. The fight was hot and heavy until finally the bomb-bay doors came open and out tumbled our bombs. We also dropped two smoke bombs. The rest of the wing dropped their loads on our smoke bombs.

We were having it rough. The fighters all seemed to be after us. They knew that if we were destroyed the whole wing would fail, because they couldn't bomb through the clouds. The air was full of flak shells and white 20 mm shells from fighters, especially in our vicinity. I swore, and fought. What else could I do.

As all things must, this ended as we left the target and turned homeward.

Bill called the crew and asked if anyone had been hit, as the ship was literally riddled like a sieve. Galba didn't answer so Beans left his waist gun and went back to see if he was OK. Galba's twin fifties (.50 caliber machine guns) were heard firing over the target. When you are in a firefight with fighters, oxygen checks of the crew are not always performed as often as they normally are. I waited impatiently for Beans to call from the tail. When he did, he sounded sad and afraid. He said Galba's oxygen hose was not connected to the supply and he was slumped over his guns. He tried to revive him and fed him pure oxygen for a long time but he wouldn't come to. I prayed like hell and couldn't bring myself to realize he might be dead, even after Beans called and said he thought he was. When we crossed the enemy coast and headed over the North Sea, we dove for the water and good air in a vain attempt to revive Galba. I left my turret and went toward the tail. They had laid him out on his back with his feet toward the nose of the ship. I crawled along the narrow passage and up over his body. My face came to a stop about six inches from his. His face was as white as snow with frozen mucous in his nose and mouth and his eyes were staring wide open into mine, all covered in frost. I took a quick gasp. I knew then he was dead. One look told me. A look that haunted me every time I closed my eyes for months afterward. I crawled half-dazed back through the plane where Beans stood by his waist gun. We looked at each other not knowing what to say. I sat down and lit a cigarette for Beans and myself and we sat in silence and smoked.

We flew directly to Alconbury as effective with this mission, pathfinder crews would return to the 482nd base for interrogation rather than fly to the base of the group they had led.

We fired a red flare as we circled to land. Everyone on the crew was upset and we made two approaches and had to go around each time. We landed roughly on the third approach and as we passed one of the runways, Al Engelhardt, who didn't go with us, waved at us. I waved back weakly.

We stopped amid a crowd of people and doctors and ambulances and I hopped out. The stretcher bearers and doctor wanted to know who was hurt and I told them the tail gunner was dead. I watched as they rolled his body out onto the stretcher and took him into the ambulance and a tear rolled down my check. I wasn't ashamed. He was my buddie.

They buried him in the American Cemetery near Cambridge, and I go there as often as I can to put fresh flowers on his grave. He was a swell fellow.

It had been a rough day and our ship was full of holes. I left for bed but couldn't sleep. Galba's bed next to mine was stripped and his clothes were taken by the quartermaster. I rolled over so I wouldn't see it.

For a long time I assumed Bill Galba had accidentally disconnected his oxygen mask. Later, I remember Bill Owen saying another problem may have contributed to Bill Galba's death. Bill Galba was reported to have a very bad ulcer, and it could have flared up, causing him to vomit into his oxygen mask, choking him.

Mission No. 8 — Bremen, Germany (December 20, 1943)

Nineteen days passed since our mission to Solingen before we were called for our next mission which was Bremen. The philosophy of the USAAF was to get airmen flying again or in combat again as soon as possible after an airplane crash or other accident in which airmen died. However, in our case after Bill Galba's death, we had a fairly long interval before we were once again in combat.

Another change in our crew occurred when Harry Stotler, waist gunner, was grounded permanently because of medical problems he suffered when flying at high altitude. All of us were sad to lose Harry, who had been one of our crew from the beginning, and a very dependable gunner, but medical decisions on flight status took precedence over all other considerations.

Harry's replacement was Harlen "Hop" Sours, a native of Luray, Virginia. Harlen had been a medic in the U.S. Army in Northern Ireland before volunteering to be an aerial gunner. He trained as a gunner in England and on completion was assigned to the 813th Bomb Squadron of the 482nd Bomb Group.

The Following Account of the Mission to Bremen, Germany, December 20, 1943, Was Written by S/Sgt. John J. O'Neil

To give some background on where replacement gunners came from, I will tell my story of how I came to be assigned the job of replacing S/Sgt. Bill Galba as tail gunner on Bill Owen's crew.

In 1941, I volunteered to do my one-year draft service and was inducted into the U.S. Army on July 3, 1941 in Boston, Massachusetts, and was shipped to Fort Devens, Ayer, Mass. At that time, a regular Army hitch was three years, and as an inducement, the Army let an enlistee pick his initial base. A Navy hitch was six years, and a Marine hitch was four years. But the one-year hitch appealed to me. At Fort Devens, we were given uniforms and Army Classification tests. The stays were very short at recruit reception centers and usually in about ten days, the new soldiers were shipped out by the hundreds all over the U.S. to forts, camps or bases for basic training. By some stroke of luck, I and another soldier, who was a pharmacist in civilian life, were sent to the Manchester Air Base (later renamed Grenier Field) in Manchester, New Hampshire and assigned to the Base Hospital Medical Detachment.

Although I did not particularly like being in the Medical Corps, the approximate year and one-half I spent at Grenier Field went by fast, and I made the most of being stationed about 50 miles from my home town of Malden, Massachusetts, a suburb of Boston.

The major event of 1941 was, of course, the Japanese attack on Pearl Harbor. After President Roosevelt declared war on Japan, and among other changes, the length-of-duty hitches went out the window as all servicemen were in for the duration. As with most other Army Air Force ground personnel the idea of being a pilot, or other member of a flight crew was very attractive to me. Unfortunately, I was not able to complete my application requirements for Aviation Cadet before leaving Grenier Field in December 1942 for Camp Kilmer, New Jersey, and eventual arrival in England and assignment to the Eighth Air Force in January 1943.

Our transport, the Queen Elizabeth I, was an extremely large ship and on each wartime crossing carried about 15,000 military personnel from New York City to Greenock, Scotland (near Glasgow) in five days. To avoid German submarines, the Q.E. I ran a zig-zag course, and coupled with its superior speed actually outran German submarines during all of its wartime crossings of the Atlantic. After debarking at Greenock we eventually made our way to a RAF air base at Debden in Essex, which was the home of the 4th Fighter Group. This group was unique in that most of its flying personnel were members of the famed RAF Eagle Squadron. These pilots had enlisted in the RAF or RCAF, and saw action in England and Europe before Pearl Harbor or before the Eighth Air Force arrived in England in 1942.

Debden was a permanent RAF station of mostly brick buildings. In early 1943 there were still some RAF personnel on base doing certain jobs, but eventually it became more American. At that time, the pilots were still flying Spitfires, but before I left Debden in May 1943, the Spitfires had been replaced with P-47 Thunderbolts, much to the dislike of the pilots, who preferred the sleek, more maneuverable Spitfire to the big, heavy P-47. My duties involved ambulance driving for the flight line, and miscellaneous other duties.

Although Debden was an interesting base, I got thinking again about how exciting it would be to become a pilot which would require applying for Aviation Cadet training. Around this time, there were announcements that volunteers were being recruited for aerial gunners to fly on B-17s and B-24s in England. Building on this, the idea developed that if one were to become an aerial gunner, and fly some combat missions, it should help one's application for cadet considerably. I thus applied to be a gunner, and passed a physical examination in London, and went off to gunnery school in May 1943.

We were sent to a RAF base at Kirkham, Lancashire for training. There were about 20-25 GIs in the class. They came from just about every part of the Army, including infantry. The ground school consisted of lectures and demonstrations on the .50 caliber machine gun, and turrets of the various bombers. After about a month, we were sent to the Central East Coast of England, to an area called the Wash. At the Wash, we shot the .50 caliber machine gun at a tow target that was pulled by a B-17 just out over the water.

FIG. 6.1. TWO P-47N THUNDERBOLT FIGHTERS FLYING IN FORMATION
The P-47 was the first USAAF fighter to successfully escort 8th Air Force bombers in
Europe and challenge the Luftwaffe.
(Courtesy of Ed Kueppers)

From the Wash, we were sent to Bovingdon airfield near London. We were given lectures on combat missions, and also had a pressure chamber exercise in which we were taken to a simulated 30,000 feet altitude, utilizing oxygen masks. To show how important oxygen was at 30,000 feet, each trainee in turn removed his mask and attempted to write on a piece of paper. As 30 seconds is the approximate survival time at that altitude, you could hardly write your name, and then you would start to lose consciousness. An attendant helped get your oxygen mask on, and you quickly recovered. Everything was fine, except the outside chamber attendant played a joke on the inside chamber attendant, and dropped the chamber altitude so quickly, I nearly busted both ear drums, and couldn't hear too well for about three weeks.

After about a week at Bovingdon, we completed the aerial gunnery course, and received a diploma indicating we were aerial gunners. However, none of the new gunners had yet been in an airplane, which of course, was a key part of aerial gunnery.

As replacement gunners, we were sent to various bomb groups. I was assigned on August 26, 1943 to the 813th Bomb Squadron, 482nd Bomb Group

(P) at Alconbury. I soon learned that the (P) stood for pathfinders, and that the group was training to do missions using radar to navigate. The first radar the Eighth Air Force had was developed by the British who at that time were ahead of us in electronics. I recall seeing in a London department store window a television, and couldn't figure out what it was. However, later on American scientists at M.I.T., building on the original British radar, developed an improved radar which was used by the Eighth for the remainder of the air war. The British radar designated H_2S was slung under the nose of the B-17 and was called a "bathtub" by the airmen. The navigator operated the radar and sat at a table in the radio room. The radio operator sat in the nose and manipulated his radio equipment and served as a nose gunner.

FIG. 6.2. AN UNIDENTIFIED FLYING OFFICER STANDING BY A P-47
SHOWING THE HUGE SIZE OF THIS FIGHTER
There are four .50 caliber machine guns in the right and left wings just above each wheel.
(Courtesy of Ed Kueppers)

At the 482nd, I was assigned to an experienced crew to replace a gunner who was in the hospital. Capt. Lyman Collins, the pilot, asked me if I had ever flown before. When I told him no, he wasn't too happy. I made a few flights, and that took care of that.

To give the 482nd BG a good sendoff, Gen Ira C. Eaker visited the base and two crews lined up in front of a radar-equipped B-17. Capt. Collins' crew was one of these crews, and I was included. Gen. Eaker came down the line, and said to each airman, "My name is Eaker, what's yours?" Gen. Eaker gave a short talk and the 482nd was ready for missions.

I flew two attempted missions (Wesel and Bremen) with Capt. Collins' crew, but due to bad weather and mechanical problems, both missions were aborted and we received no credit. About this time, I was transferred to another crew (Lt. Owen) which turned out to be a fortunate move for me, as several weeks later, Capt. Collins and crew took a direct flak hit over Frankfurt, and all were lost.

Our mission routine differed from that of the typical bomb group, in that a crew would be alerted in the late afternoon, and some time during the evening would fly with bombs to another bomb group base to serve as the pathfinder lead for the next day's mission.

On December 19, 1943, an alert was posted on the 813th bulletin board for Lt. Owen's crew to fly a mission the next day. As there was not enough room in the several gunners' barracks, I and another replacement gunner, Herschel McCoy, were housed in a barracks which had mostly radar mechanics. About 10 P.M., Sgt. Culp came to our barracks and told me to report to Operations/Equipment as we were going on a mission. For me the wake-up call to go on a mission was something that was always difficult to get used to. I didn't know Lt. Owen's crew, but they were friendly and helpful to me as a novice gunner. We were not briefed at our home base, because the target for the next day's mission was top secret. After getting all of our equipment together, we were taken by truck out to our B-17. The ground crew had our guns at the ship but the gunners always installed them. In that way the gunners felt more comfortable and were responsible for the installation. We usually carried six 500-pound high explosive bombs and smoke bombs or flares. Our bomb loads were lighter than the other planes on a mission, as we needed more flexibility.

We took off for our assigned base and landed in about one-half hour without incident. Flying around blacked-out England with bombs was an eerie feeling. Our pilots and navigator were excellent in finding strange air bases in total darkness. Though an early evening takeoff and landing at an assigned bomber base would have given the Pathfinder crews a chance to sleep, it always seemed we arrived in the wee hours of the morning and were lucky to catch a few winks.

Wake-up time was about 3 A.M., and then to breakfast. A combat breakfast was a special treat of bacon and fried eggs (which were unobtainable otherwise), pancakes and coffee, Then briefing, and we learned the target on the map was Bremen, also known as "Little B" in deference to "Big B" (Berlin). The briefing officer went over the expected enemy fighters and antiaircraft guns which were moderately heavy. The weather officer predicted less than complete cloud cover. Of 546 bombers taking off, 472 B-17 and B-24 bombers would take part in the mission, and our fighter escort included 491 P-47s, P-51s and P-38s.

We took off about 8 A.M. and groups and wings joined up over England, and continued to climb to an altitude of 26,000 feet over the North Sea. Then gunners checked their guns with short bursts. This was my first mission flying in the tail position, and I tried to keep Bill Owen and the crew informed on the rest of the formation. We had no contact with enemy fighters on the route to the target. However, on reaching Bremen, all hell broke loose. Flak shells were bursting everywhere and we were attacked by German twin- engine fighters firing rockets at our formation. I saw a B-17 take a direct hit and burst into flames. That B-17 couldn't have burned faster if it was made of paper. Enemy fighters and our escort fighters were locked in combat all over the sky. A Messerschmitt 110 attacked us from a six o'clock high position and I got off a

FIG. 6.3. A P-51 MUSTANG — THE BEST USAAF FIGHTER OF WWII
In addition to superior flight characteristics, the P-51 had the longest range
of all USAAF fighters.
(Courtesy of Ed Kueppers)

FIG. 6.4. THE P-38 LIGHTNING — THIS FIGHTER WAS USED TO A LIMITED
EXTENT BY THE EIGHTH
The P-38 was unusual in that it had twin engines and twin fuselages.
(Courtesy of Ed Kueppers)

couple of bursts. George Moffat in the ball turret picked up this fighter on his Sperry gunsight and got off bursts which sent the fighter down in a spin. George was officially credited with a destroyed Me-110. After what seemed like a never-ending flak barrage, I heard Marshall Thixton say, "Bombs Away." When flak is real close, you can see the red color as the shells explode, and also hear a loud thumping noise.

After leaving the Bremen area, Bill Owen called me on the intercom and asked if I could see any damage to our ship. I told him no. As we had taken flak damage in the right waist area of the plane, Bill Owen came down to about 15,000 feet, and left the formation. About this time, George Moffat came crawling back in the tail to tell me to come up to the waist area as we might have to make a parachute jump! Remembering lectures on the subject, I recalled survival time in the North Sea in winter to be about 30 minutes. So far I had seen just about everything on my first mission and it wasn't over yet.

On reaching the waist, I saw a large flak hole in the upper right waist plus numerous other smaller holes. Don White, our flight engineer, was holding as best he could the two ends of the right control cables which the flak had severed. Fortunately, the left control cables remained intact. We were over the North Sea on a direct heading for England, but about 300 miles from home. We huddled between the waist and radio room as Bill Owen and Frank McAllister did their best to keep us on a steady course. Thankfully, we finally saw the English Coast, and now all we had to worry about was our landing. Bill Owen told everyone to go to the radio room which was the usual crew crash landing position in a B-17. Bill and Mac did not know how the ship would take the landing, but as it turned out, it was a smooth landing.

At interrogation, all flight personnel were given one shot of Scotch whisky and other refreshments. We learned that the German Air Force also bombed our bomber formations. According to 482nd records, all 12 Pathfinder aircraft received flak damage, confirming reports of intense and accurate flak. And excellent bombing results were reported through clouds of one-tenth to seven-tenths. Half of the Pathfinders bombed on radar and half bombed visually. In the *Mighty Eighth War Diary* (Freeman *et al.* 1990), it is recorded that the Eighth lost 27 bombers and 6 fighters that day.

I was thankful to survive my first mission and to voice the sentiment that the nickname of "Little B" for Bremen was an understatement.

CHRISTMAS — DECEMBER 25, 1943

The Following Account was a Collaborative Effort by S/Sgts. John J. O'Neil and George E. Moffat

Maybe it was the song: "I'll Be Home For Christmas...," but many GIs referred to when they would get home in terms of "this Christmas," or more commonly "next Christmas," especially in the early years of the war. And in terms of the alternative of spending Christmas away from home, there was a lot of effort on everyone's part to make it as much as possible like the Christmases we knew back home. The cooks did their utmost to serve a traditional Christmas dinner, including turkey and stuffing, mashed potatoes, vegetables, and apple and mince pies.

Our shoebox type gift packages from home increased in number around Christmas time and in addition to cookies, fruit cake, and candy items, we received useful gifts of socks, handkerchiefs and underwear, which were very difficult to obtain in England.

Special religious services were held for the Eighth personnel, and on December 24, 1943 there was a midnight Mass celebrated in the building that served as our movie theater, and it was well-attended.

George Moffat really got into the Christmas spirit. On Christmas morning he dug down in his barracks bag and found a considerable number of cigarette packs that he had accumulated since leaving the U.S. He headed for the small nearby Alconbury village and went to each house and left a few packs of Chesterfield cigarettes. A number of the residents felt obliged to invite George in for a drink, and by the time the Chesterfields ran out, George was feeling mighty good.

Another common happening at Eighth bases during the Christmas season was to hold Christmas parties for local children where the GIs would "adopt" a child for the party. At Alconbury, for Christmas 1943, the combat crews' mess hall was decorated and also had a Christmas tree in readiness for the big event.

Our recollection is that our crew was alerted for a mission on Christmas day, but it was scrubbed, and, in fact, no USAAF missions were flown that day, and thus the war was forgotten briefly.

In the early afternoon of Christmas day, after the main dinner meal was completed, the children and chaperons were trucked to Alconbury for the party. We even had a Santa Claus and the airmen and the children played games, enjoyed refreshments, and finally the children received presents from Santa. The children certainly enjoyed the festivities and the GIs almost felt like they were back home with their families.

Mission No. 9 — Ludwigshafen (December 30, 1943)
The Following Account Was Written by Lt. Marshall J. Thixton

On December 29, 1943, our crew was alerted for a mission. We were to lead the 390th Bomb Group, and per procedure, we flew to the 390BG base at Framlingham the night before the mission, arriving slightly after 1:30 a.m. Bill Owen had to ask the 390th to turn on the landing lights so we could land. They took us to temporary quarters and we got a little sleep before being awakened around 4:00 A.M. for our briefing.

The target was Ludwigshafen, which was far into Germany, and as usual when we saw the string on the map stretching well across Germany, the groans of the combat crews could be heard all through the briefing room.

We took off at 6:00 A.M., assembled our group and started climbing to our bombing altitude of 28,000 feet. This higher altitude we liked, because flak and fighters were not as dangerous as they were at 25,000 or below, or at least that is what we told ourselves. Our P-47s escorted us to just inside the German border. As our fighters left us to return to England, we were attacked by about 30-40 German fighters: mostly FW-190s and Me-109s. The Germans had learned if they attacked our formations head-on, they could come in 100 to 200 feet high, and B-17 chin-turret guns could not fire that high. It was tough seeing them come straight in and not be able to fire a shot at them. Of course, our top-turret guns could reach them and I heard Sgt. Don White's guns blazing away, and as they came down through the formation, the ball-turret guns could pick them up. Our speed of about 150 mph and their closing speed of about 300 mph made the time they were under fire a very short time, only a few seconds.

At least we were getting closer to the target, although it seemed like hours. Heavy flak started coming up as we approached the target, and I opened the bomb-bay doors and when given the release signal, I dropped the bombs and quickly closed the bomb-bay doors and got back to my guns, because I knew as we left the target and flak area, the German fighters would be back and they were, but not as many as before, and we kept them at a distance.

FIG. 6.5. A FW-190 LUFTWAFFE FIGHTER AND PILOTS ON THE ALERT WAITING
TO ATTACK EIGHTH AIR FORCE BOMBERS AND FIGHTERS
The FW-190 and Me-109 were the most effective German fighters in WWII.
(Courtesy of Ian Hawkins)

Bombing was done through 10/10 cloud cover, and the results were good. Some crews observed black smoke rising through the clouds at the target area according to the 482nd History.

We headed home, and eventually arrived at the beautiful English coastline. We relaxed for the first time in what seemed like forever, even though we were over Germany for only about four hours. We landed in Alconbury, and went to interrogation, were given our shot of Scotch whisky, and related the details of the mission. I then headed for bed, where I remained for about 12 hours.

The details of the mission as given by Freeman *et al.* (1990) were that a total of 658 B-17s and B-24s participated in the mission and 23 bombers were lost. The escorting fighters numbered 583, and 13 of these were lost.

The Following Account of the Mission to Ludwigshafen, Germany, December 30, 1943, Was Written by S/Sgt. George E. Moffat

Just before Christmas, we rested plenty the next few days. And went on a two-day pass to London, where we had a good time and tried to forget about the war in general. We went to a good show, ate in the best restaurants and stayed at the Piccadilly Hotel. When night fell, we hit the hot-spots and raised cain until the wee small hours. Then when we could hold our eyes open no longer, we climbed into a taxi and went back to the hotel where we slept till 11 A.M. the next day.

After breakfast in bed, we bathed and dressed in freshly-pressed clothes that the valet had done for us. We left to see London. A complete tour was made, including the Tower of London, Madame Tussauds Wax Museum, St. Paul's, Westminster Abbey and the Houses of Parliament. We spent a very enjoyable day and that evening after supper, we repeated our actions of the previous night.

We thought about staying for another day to spend Christmas Eve in town, but our cash was dangerously low and besides we didn't know if we would be alerted Christmas Eve, so we decided to go back to base. And also we had our children's Christmas party and festivities to attend. The next morning we went to Kings Cross Station and caught the 9:20 train to Huntingdon. On coming back to Alconbury, we looked forward to some good grub and plenty of it. Good food in London was hard to get, even at the best places.

After the excitement of Christmas was over we began looking forward to the New Year. It seemed funny to be saying 1944. But on December 30th we were fated to give Adolf an old year's last kiss. The night before they awakened us a little after midnight and we left for a briefing. We were to lead the 390th Group, so after loading our guns on the plane we took off, landing at the 390th a little past 1:30 A.M. We were disappointed that we couldn't lead our old 95th outfit, but there wasn't very much we could do about it. We had time to lie down for only a short time. We had no sooner arrived by truck at a barracks, when it seemed we had to get ready and go to breakfast.

It didn't take us long to eat and we left for briefing. In a room similar to that at the 95th, full of maps, etc., the crews sat, smoking and chewing the fat. Soon a major came in and the room quieted down, as he unveiled the map revealing the tape running to Ludwigshafen, and seemingly very close to a number of flak areas. It was a long haul. We were to have fighter protection about one-third of the way in and the British Spitfires were to meet us on the way out as far inside the enemy coastline as their fuel would allow. Flak over the target was to be heavy and about 400 assorted fighters could reach us. Bombing altitude was 28,000 feet. After briefing, we left for our ship and installed our guns.

At 6 A.M., we took off carrying a load of 500-lb bombs and two smoke bombs. At 20,000 feet we assembled the group and I sat in the radio room day-dreaming. As we left the coast, I climbed into my turret and looked things over. Everything checked out okay so I sat, going slowly around, watching the rest of the ships behind us and catching glimpses of the water below through the clouds. I spotted a convoy of 34 ships and reported it on intercom.

We encountered no flak as we passed the enemy coast and our fighter cover looked swell. There were about 50 or so P-47s circling all around us. I wished to God they could stay with us all the way. But as we entered Germany proper they swung off and headed home.

FIG. 6.6. GENERAL ADOLF GALLAND (LEFT), MOST FAMOUS GERMAN FIGHTER
ACE, AND HIS WINGMAN FLYING ME-109Fs
Whenever there were German fighters on the attack,
the Me-109s were right in the middle of it.
(Courtesy of Raymond F. Toliver and Trevor J. Constable)

The P-47s had no sooner left than a flock of FW-190s, Me-109s, and -110s jumped us. About 40 altogether. They livened things up for us and I completely forgot I was tired. A slug or something made a zing and whistle as it tore through a side window of my turret. I ducked instinctively. Fighter cannon shells made white puffs, like deadly snowballs, which crept closer, one after the other, toward us. The ship jumped crazily when a shell exploded close by.

I got a bead on a 190 going past down below us and peppered him good, but he didn't go down. As I swung my turret up I saw a FW-190 coming head on at us followed by a 109 and I held my guns down on them. One trailed some black smoke, but as I watched he climbed back up into the fight.

FIG. 6.7. TWIN-ENGINE ME-110s WITH ROCKET LAUNCHERS
The Me-110 was an all-purpose fighter used for launching rockets at 8th bombers, attacking straggling bombers that had left the formations, and occasionally attacking bomber formations directly.
(Courtesy of Ian Hawkins)

Out of the corner of my eye, I saw something move and swung around to 12 o'clock. There was a Me-110 seemingly suspended right in front of me at about 200 yards. Dead meat. I poured everything I had into him and he dove. I kept firing as he dove, and after about a thousand feet down, I lost him.

The bomb-bay doors came open and flak came up. It was an extremely heavy barrage and they certainly had our altitude down pat. The ship rocked and shook under the impacts, and the whistle of flak as it pinged through the fuselage made me more nervous. Made everyone nervous. The bombs left and I heard a terrific boom. I thought "Oh God" and looked at my arms and felt my legs to see if they were still there. I thought sure my turret had received a direct hit. I found out later it was the smoke bombs exploding some feet below me. Funny I had never heard them before.

The flak came up heavy until we left the city and then the fighters hit us again. It was rough. At last our fighters came and Jerry beat it. We were sure thankful for the help our "little friends" gave us.

We made it back okay and landed with numerous flak holes in the ship. The mechanics were trying to count them. Then to interrogation, chow and a well-deserved sack where we remained for 20 hours.

FIG. 6.8. RADAR VIPs VISIT ALCONBURY DECEMBER 1943
Left to right: Col. Lawrence, 482nd BG Commanding Officer, Lord Cherwell, Chief Scientific Advisor to Prime Minister Churchill, Col. Garland, 8th Air Force Headquarters, Dave Griggs, Advisor to Secretary of War Stimson, Sir Robert Watson Watt, Acknowledged to be the Inventor of British Radar.
(Courtesy of Mrs. Kay Engelhardt)

CHAPTER 7

NEW YEAR'S EVE – DECEMBER 31, 1943

JOHN J. O'NEIL
GEORGE E. MOFFAT

The Following Account Was Written by S/Sgt. John J. O'Neil

After our December 30th raid to Ludwigshafen, we were fortunate in not being scheduled to fly a mission again until January 4, 1944. This break allowed any of our crew who wanted to celebrate New Year's Eve to go into town to do so. As enlisted members of our crew were not all housed together in the same barracks, when it was time to go to town, most of them went in different directions.

The town of Alconbury was very small and had only one pub (public house), so not too many GIs went there. I don't remember ever going to the very small town of Alconbury, other than riding my bicycle through there maybe once.

Huntingdon was a fair-sized town which was about five miles from our base, and thus reachable by bicycle, as well as by the occasional public transportation bus (same one that went to Cambridge) and GI truck. Huntingdon had a movie, a Red Cross Club that served coke and donuts, a few pubs, and restaurants, and a drug store. The drug store was important because it had a film-developing service. Army regulations forbade photographing any military equipment or facility, but taking pictures of friends and civilian scenes was a popular pastime of many GIs.

The two nearest good-sized towns were Cambridge and Peterborough. Of the two, I preferred Cambridge, which had a couple of movie theaters, a few good restaurants, a number of good pubs, and a Red Cross that served donuts and coke. Some Red Cross locations also had sleeping facilities (bunk or double-bunk beds), but these were in the very large cities, such as London and Edinburgh, Scotland.

Cambridge was located about 17 miles from Alconbury. A public transportation bus passed our base around 3:00 P.M., at least on weekdays, and was a convenient way to get to Cambridge. The ride was enjoyable, but about half-way between Alconbury and Cambridge, there was a building by the side of the road that had a very large sign which read: CREMATORIUM. On passing this foreboding building, I did not have pleasant thoughts on what went on within its walls. It was also possible to get a ride in a GI truck from our base motor pool about 5:00 P.M. directly to Cambridge. The back-to-Alconbury truck left Cambridge about 11:30 P.M., and if you missed it, that meant you stayed someplace in Cambridge, as there was no public transportation to Alconbury in the evening.

After a number of trips to Cambridge, I developed a sort of routine. If possible, I would take the public transportation bus to Cambridge as it got one there earlier in the afternoon. On one of the main streets in Cambridge was a small restaurant that was run by a woman who seemed to be a refugee of sorts from some country in Europe. In any case it was about the only restaurant that I ever found in England where one could order a fried egg — a goose egg. As fresh eggs were unobtainable, those goose eggs really hit the spot. After a filling meal at my favorite restaurant, I would often go to the movies, which was back toward the central part of Cambridge. There was usually only one feature picture shown at the movie theater along with a 10-minute world news. The news usually featured some aspect of what British forces were doing around the world, and often highlighted results achieved by General Montgomery's army. This was described by GIs and others somewhat jokingly as, "Monty does it again."

After leaving the movie, it was only a short walk to my favorite pub. The pub was located one floor below ground level, and above the entrance door was a door bell that would ring down in the pub, and the pubkeeper would, if so inclined, operate a mechanism that would allow the entrance door to be opened. There were no outside pub signs and thus most passersby wouldn't even know there was a pub one flight of stairs down.

The pub (I think it was the Prince of Wales) was run by an English lady in her forties and her mother. They were wonderful people and very friendly to the Americans who happened to know how to find the place. It seemed as if many of the regulars were always in attendance. One of the regulars was an attractive English lady of about 50 whose husband was a RAF pilot, who had been shot down on a night mission to Germany. As I recall she had been notified that he was missing in action, but she never gave up hope that he would turn up as a prisoner of war or escapee. I never did finally learn his fate. She was a schoolmarm type and to my knowledge always left the pub with her other lady friends and never dated any of the many and varied military personnel who frequented the pub.

Another regular was George, who was then in the British Home Guard. Almost everyone in England during WWII worked in some sort of military job or war effort. The Home Guard was a form of civilian defense, and were called upon during air raids or other disasters. George was a WWI veteran, and it was always enjoyable to talk to him about old times over a mild and bitters (beer).

On New Year's Eve four of us, including a gunner from another crew, two radar mechanics and I caught the bus to Cambridge. Among many combat crews, there was a philosophy of eat, drink and be merry, because tomorrow you may die. Being a member of an 8th Air Force combat crew, one had many advantages over other soldiers and sailors in combat, for example, you lived on a base in a civilized country, could sleep in a regular bunk bed, eat regular meals, go to movies, go shopping, eat in restaurants, have contact with civilians, and do most things civilians do. Yet when you left your base to fly on a mission to enemy territory, all of that changed suddenly, and you could be shot down and killed, thus fulfilling the prophecy that tomorrow you may die.

We went to my favorite restaurant and had an enjoyable meal. Although in wartime England, good food was hard to find, it was always a pleasure to get away from mess-hall food. England was famous for its fish and chips stores, where for a reasonable sum, a fairly good fried fish and about a pound of French fries, all wrapped up in newspapers, could be had.

We then headed for the downstairs pub. It was always enjoyable to get out of the damp, winter chill of blacked-out England into the warm, friendly atmosphere of a pub. There were more people than usual celebrating, including many strangers to me. We drank mild and bitters beer and talked about many things, including other New Year's Eve experiences.

Whiskey or other spirits' drinks were generally not available in wartime English pubs. Supposedly each pub was allotted one bottle (a fifth) of Scotch per day, and of course, this precious ration was served to only the most preferred customers. We were especially fortunate as our pubkeeper, Dorothy, gave each of us one shot of Scotch. The hitch was that the shot of Scotch was mixed in with a glass of mild and bitters, so that no one could see that you were being favored with Scotch. I can assure you this is not the best way to drink Scotch.

Pubs were really smoke-filled rooms, as almost everyone, whether military or civilians, smoked cigarettes. I always carried at least two packs of American cigarettes when going to town, as we were generous in offering them to civilians, especially English girls. English cigarettes could be bought, but they were expensive and of poor quality. In any case, no one ever complained of second-hand smoke.

During the course of the evening, we noticed four young ladies who were together at a table. As it was always more fun to talk and drink beer with female companions, we asked if we could join them and they said yes.

English girls always asked American soldiers where they came from, hoping the answer would be Hollywood. It seemed that most of the movies shown in English movie theaters were made in America, and Hollywood was, therefore, the most important place in the United States. There was also a belief by the English that most people in America were quite well-to-do financially and this could be discussed back and forth at some length.

English pubs had one serious disadvantage, namely, about 9:50 P.M. the pubkeeper would shout, "Time Gentlemen, Time," which meant in 10 minutes, the pub had to close for the night. Another rule for pubs was no beer was to be taken out of the pub. We usually went along with this rule, but this once we ordered extra bottles of beer and stashed them in our overcoats, as we wanted to continue our party beyond ten o'clock.

After leaving the pub, we and our four ladyfriends strolled around Cambridge in the blackout, chatting and sipping on our beer. Cambridge was home to the famous universities which were housed there, and many students and their dates were out celebrating. We found a restaurant open and decided it was time to get something to eat. The hot tea and cakes were just fine and soon it was about 11:45 P.M.

We left the restaurant and at midnight some bells rang, we all kissed and said Happy New Year! Our GI truck ride was scheduled to leave for Alconbury at 12:30 A.M., which we just caught in time after saying goodbye to our lady friends and promising to look for them again in the pub.

The Following Account was Written by S/Sgt. George E. Moffat

We awakened late in the afternoon of the 31st of December. This was New Year's Eve coming up and we were quite determined to raise a good bit of devilment. The best place to do that of course is London so we hurried into our clothes. I loaned Don White a pair of pants, because his were both unpressed and we had no time to do it if we were going to catch that 6:35 train at Huntingdon which was 5 miles or so away. Without eating we dashed out, unshaven and very crummy looking to say the least, planning on sprucing up after arriving in London. We caught a passing jeep and he was going right through Huntingdon. Boy! That was one of the wildest rides I've ever been on. That corporal should have been drawing flight pay. We only touched the road about every 300 yards. Anyway he had us there at 6:30. The train was early and already waiting at the platform. We ran through the gates, each pointing in turn to the following man as the ticket taker put out his hand for tickets we didn't have time to purchase. White was last through and called back, "We'll get them at the other end so ta-ta," and we climbed on board as the train began to move.

The train journey was uneventful, at least for most of us. White had met a girl and was talking her ear off and he disappeared when we arrived at Kings Cross, so we figured his talking had soaked in, and we left for a hotel. The train had us in at 8:45 so we had most of the evening ahead of us. First of all we went and had some food, as we were nearly starved. Our last meal was almost 40 hours ago and I guess the poor waiter thought it had been 40 years. We nearly wore his legs off to the hips dragging tray after tray to our table while the English customers in the place sat watching us with eyes as big as saucers. The proof of our appetite came for the six of us in the form of a check for 7 pounds, 10 shillings (about $30 which was a lot in those days).

After stuffing ourselves sufficiently we managed to walk to the door and hail a taxi and went to the Imperial Hotel in Russell Square, where knowing the desk girls fairly well I managed to acquire three double rooms in the "supposedly" full hotel. We shaved and washed while the valet pressed our clothes and then hit the street raring to go at precisely 11 P.M.

We wandered from place to place, finally ending up at the Patomac Club for the midnight celebration. We had a very good time and after the crowd began to dwindle at 3:00 A.M. we hooked a ride back to the hotel on a newspaper wagon. We then hit the hay for the first time in 1944.

The next morning we arose rather late and had lunch, saw a show and caught a 4 o'clock train back to Huntingdon. We got our pay out of the 813th orderly room and paid Bill Owen and Al Engelhardt back 15 pounds each.

CHANGE IN CREW

Around this time, we had a change in our crew. T/Sgt. Lloyd Cain, who had been wounded by flak in the Munster raid, was relieved from combat for medical reasons. Though a character, he had performed his duties as Radio Operator/Gunner in an efficient manner, and was our only crew member to receive a Purple Heart. It was always tough to lose an original crew member for any reason.

T/Sgt. Edmund R. Aken, of Elkville, Illinois, was our new Radio Operator/Gunner. He became our senior crew member by age as he was in his early thirties. He had a friendly personality and a portly build, and soon became the well-liked, fatherly-type member of our crew. In addition, he was a first-rate radio technician.

CHAPTER 8

AIR COMBAT: 482ND BOMB GROUP (P)
KIEL — FRANKFURT — LEIPZIG — FRANKFURT

MARSHALL J. THIXTON
GEORGE E. MOFFAT
JOHN J. O'NEIL

The holiday season was over and it was back to business in earnest. Big changes occurred in the Eighth Air Force Headquarters with General Eaker being transferred to Italy to head the Allied Mediterranean Air Forces and General Doolittle coming to England to command the Eighth Air Force. General Eaker was very unhappy with this development, but he was unable to change the decision, and as a good soldier, dutifully reported to his new headquarters in Italy. Many of the airmen of the Eighth could not understand the reasons for the change either, particularly as the Eighth was gaining in numbers of men and planes, and in a few months time, it is generally conceded that the Luftwaffe was in its final decline. It didn't make sense that as General Eaker and the men of the Eighth from mid-1942 had carried the air war against Germany, often with understaffing in men and planes, and as the final showdown prior to D-Day was unfolding, it was necessary to bring General Doolittle from Africa to lead the final charge.

Mission No. 10 — Kiel, Germany (January 4, 1944)

The Following Account of the Mission to Kiel, Germany, January 4, 1944, was Written by S/Sgt. George E. Moffat

On the evening of January 3rd we were called by Sgt. Culp before going to bed to report to operations in twenty minutes, so we got our .45s out and got into our coveralls. Dachuck remarked as I dressed that he wanted my blouse if I went down and I won't record here what my retort was.

We walked up to "Ops" and hung around smoking until we were told what field we were to go to and when to take off. We were leading the 100th Bomb Group, also known as the "Clay Pigeons" of the 8th Air Force, because of their high losses on missions.

We took off from Alconbury at midnight and checked our guns over as we flew to the 100th BG base. We landed about 12:30 A.M. and rode in to operations where they fixed us up with bunks for a few hours sleep. At 3 A.M. we were awakened and left for breakfast where we met two guys whom we had trained with and flew over here with. There were very few of the original Major Snow Group left now and we really danced around each other. They have since been killed. The fresh eggs were good and the coffee hot. We talked over old times with them. I forget now what their names were. I believe Smithy was one. At 4 o'clock we climbed into one of the waiting trucks and went out to the equipment room with some of the old friends. When we were finished checking over our gear, we sat around talking and playing cards until the briefing room opened at 4:45. As usual I lost at the cards. I believe someone put a curse on me when I was young as far as cards go. But I went in the hole only 8 shillings, so I wasn't too disappointed, only thankful that we didn't play for 3 hours.

We gathered around the briefing room, smoking, talking and waiting for 5 o'clock to roll around. I began to think, as I sat there looking at the veiled target map, about everyone at home and what they were doing right now as I was about to go on a raid. It would be 11:00 P.M. at home. The snow would be crisp and white outside, and inside there would be a big fire in the fireplace and Mom would be shooing Bob and June off to bed. I got a bit homesick for a minute. It's funny that you will invariably become that way before you go on a raid, and yet it's not hard to understand. My train of thought was broken by the arrival of a lieutenant colonel who, it seemed, was to brief us on the mission. He was short and very fat and the guys quieted down as he began to talk. He sounded for all the world like Donald Duck. He gave us a pep talk and then unveiled the map. It was Kiel! A fairly long trip and quite a hot spot. A total of 300 twin and single-engine fighters were within intercepting range and a considerable number of flak guns were to be under us at the target, and all were very efficiently manned as I had already thought. We were to fly at an altitude of 29,000 feet at a temperature of 52 degrees below zero. Our course both in and out was routed on the map over water all the way, except for the trip across Denmark, where there would be little opposition until we actually got near the target. If we could get through the flurry of fighters and flak at the target, the remainder of the mission would be comparatively simple.

After briefing was over, we left for our ship and installed and rechecked our guns and armed the bombs. We were to start engines at 6:30, and I don't know how anyone roused women up at this time of day, but at 6:15 up rolls a Red Cross truck full of girls and coffee and doughnuts. As we had finished breakfast not so long ago we ate little, but drank 3 or 4 cups of coffee and chewed the fat with the girls. One was from Grand Rapids, Michigan so I cornered her and we literally wept on each other's shoulder at being so damn far from home. Bill whistled out the window to tell us it was starting time so we grabbed a last handful of doughnuts, not only because we were going to eat them, but because they were free, and climbed into the ship. The engines were revving up as we sat in the waist looking first at each other and then out the window at the first streaks of dawn showing off in the east, toward Germany.

Then a lurch as the brakes were released and we began to taxi out of the hardstand and onto the perimeter track toward the runway. The usual groups of mechanics and Red Cross girls waved to us as we taxied by until we came to the runway where the ships were lined up ready for takeoff. Then one by one the ships began to roar down the runway and lift up into the early morning sky. With a prayer in our hearts now, we began our roll and gathered speed. I thought she was never going to leave the ground but finally that smooth feeling came and I knew we were in the air, and we banked eastward toward Germany. As we gained our altitude, ships of the 100th came and fell in behind us in formation. At 24,000 feet we leveled off and made for Splasher #6 for the rendezvous with the rest of the wing. About four of us sat in the radio room where it was warmer and nearly fell asleep for about half an hour, until we were leaving the Coast. I made a scramble for my turret and got in, made my checks and began searching the water far below for vessels. Boy it was cold. I swore when this war was over I'd move down to the Equator. My rear extremities were numb as there is no heat element there, only the bare cloth and 1/4 in. of 40 degree below zero steel seat. My eyes were frosted and I was chattering in spite of having my electric heated suit turned on full. And now we were going up another 5,000 ft where it would be 52 degrees below. Nuts!

It seemed like hours before we finally even sighted the coast of Holland and we still had 200 miles to go before we got to the Danish Coast. I never swore so vehemently and so long before in my life at Hitler. As briefed, we saw no opposition crossing Denmark, then as we passed out over the Baltic sea we cut directly south and bore down on Kiel, only 50 miles away now. Far down below clouds were becoming dense. Vapor trails from the ships behind us streamed out like sky writers. Everything seemed outwardly peaceful. Inwardly it was seething. So was I. My God I was cold and cramped and fed up. That's a nice thing about high altitude bombing, by the time you reach your objective you are so miserably fed up you don't particularly give a damn whether you "get it" or not.

The navigator was talking to the bombardier now telling him we were only 11 miles away from the target. I continued to search the sky for enemy aircraft and as usual my efforts were rewarded. I spotted several specks off over the city and then several more. I warned the crew and sat tensely waiting for them to come. Flak began coming up from the city ahead, as the enemy fighters began diving through our formation. I poured a long burst at a FW-190 as he swooped up from below, saw him fall off and twisting down. Then we entered the flak, which was quite heavy and darned accurate. Curse those lousy devils. The bomb-bay doors began to open and I waited for "Bombs Away" as the flak poured up. An explosion right beneath me blew me right off my seat giving my head an awful crack on the top of my sights. I saw all different colors and some black too as I shook my head. The bombs began dropping out and I followed them as they began to point noses down and sail for the clouds below. It was then I began to feel my fingers getting numb. I felt for my switch but it was on full. My feet had begun to get cold also. I looked around and found a small hole by my left ribs in the plexiglass and my wire connection between my glove and suit was severed. The electric suits are wired in series and if one glove goes out, the other one and both shoes go also. I knew I couldn't stay long without freezing my hands and legs, or rather feet, but even as we passed out of the flak there were still some fighters out there. If I left my guns, the lives of my crew were at stake, so I stayed. My hands and feet were numb now and aching like mad as we turned westward across Denmark. I continued pounding my fists against my guns and my feet on the floor in an effort to regain my circulation. The pain was maddening and almost unbearable. Tears streamed down my face over my oxygen mask and froze.

In a while we passed over the Danish coast and began letting down in altitude as the fighters turned back toward their devastated city. I was nearly ready to quit and welcome death. As the danger left us I crawled out of my turret and into the waist room and asked Beans to give me a new glove or plug or something. He took off his own as we were at 20,000 ft then and stripping off my broken glove put his on my hand, which was a whitish blue color. I plugged in again and the heat made my feet and hands ache so that I had to shut my eyes and grit my teeth to keep from screaming.

Then as we passed over England, we lit cigarettes, and even I felt a lot better. On landing I was carted off to the hospital where I spent three days listening to nurses telling me how lucky I was that my hands and feet weren't frozen. The whole crew came to see me and was swell. The looks in their eyes were enough. They wanted to bawl me out for not leaving my guns, but their eyes were grateful. They're a swell gang. Anyway I'm as good as ever, and flying again.

The Following Account on the Mission to Kiel, Germany Was Written by S/Sgt. John J. O'Neil

Another aspect of pathfinder missions was the uncertain makeup of our crew after the briefing at the base of the bomb group we would lead for the mission. Usually a high-ranking officer from the lead group would fly as mission commander in the co-pilot's seat of the pathfinder ship. I recall on one mission having a general on board. Mac, our co-pilot, would give up his seat and scrunch his way through the mission, making sure he had a connection for his oxygen supply, and an occasional place at least to sit. It was entirely possible that a pathfinder co-pilot could also be bumped out of his seat and also the mission itself.

Often somebody at the group being led would decide that a pilot should ride in the tail-gunner's position on the pathfinder airplane, and keep the command pilot and pathfinder pilot informed on the formations of bombers following. Thus on the Kiel mission, I was left behind at the 100th Bomb Group when the B-17s took off. Hoppy Sours, Ellsworth Beans, and I had a rotation system for who would stay behind on a mission when our tail position was taken by a pilot, which was about as fair a resolution as possible.

In the majority of the H_2X radar-equipped B-17s, the radome was located in the ball-turret position and these airplanes thus had no ball turret, eliminating the need for a ball-turret gunner. This was not so much a problem for our crew as we flew most of our daylight missions in the H_2S radar planes, which had the radome slung under the nose.

The 100th Bomb Group was a hard-luck group that experienced more than their share of losses on missions. There was a saying that the large "D" on the tail stood for "dollar," and that your life on a 100th BG mission was not worth a dollar. Another story was that the German Air Force looked for the 100th BG on missions and attacked them in some sense of retribution, because on one mission a 100th gunner supposedly shot at a German pilot who had parachuted. (After the war, this version was discounted by heads of the German Air Force.) The Luftwaffe based their decisions on which groups to attack presumably on which bomb groups were in a given air space, whether or not there was friendly fighter escort close-by and whether the bomber formations were tight or loose, and if loose, watch out. For sure, whenever an Eighth bomber was a straggler trying to make it back to England on its own, the German fighters would circle the straggler with unrelenting attacks until the straggler went down. The only thing that could save a straggling bomber was a quick appearance of friendly fighters.

As I hung around the 100th BG base that day, many of these thoughts went through my mind. Would the German fighters go after the group with the square "D" on the tail and our pathfinder ship with no tail markings that was leading the whole formation? The hours dragged and finally the drone of bombers close-by meant the 100th planes were returning. I joined the many others at the base searching the sky to try and recognize our ship and count the number of planes returning. Sure enough, there was our pathfinder ship peeling off to land first, and fortunately all 100th BG planes returned safely.

According to the 482nd BG records, the bombing results at Kiel were good with bursts observed in the north center of the city and smoke seen rising to 3,000 feet. In the target area three twin-engine enemy aircraft fired rockets at the Eighth bombers. There was excellent fighter escort which held down the German fighter attacks. The flak at Kiel was moderate and 7 of 12 pathfinders had minor battle damage due to flak.

Freeman *et al.* (1990) reported there were 17 Eighth bombers lost out of
a total of 486, and of the 112 Eighth fighters participating, 2 were shot down.

Mission No. 11 — Frankfurt, Germany (February 4, 1944)

We had a long rest since our last mission to Kiel on January 4, 1944 and
our next scheduled mission on January 31, 1944 to Frankfurt. Our crew went
through the usual pre-mission procedure, including flying to the bomber group
we were to lead, only to have the mission scrubbed because of bad weather. At
this rate the war could be over before we complete our 25 missions. I was still
one or two missions behind Bill Owen, and my attempts to get another mission
with another crew were not successful.

Just a few days later on February 3rd, we were alerted for February 4th.
Since coming to the 482nd Bomb Group, our navigator, Al Engelhardt, had been
training on the use of radar, and now for this mission was back with us flying
his first mission as a radar navigator. It was great to have Al back on our crew,
as we always felt better when Al was doing our navigating.

This February 4th mission to Frankfurt was noteworthy as the 482nd lost
two pathfinder bombers and crews. One of these crews was led by Capt. Lyman
I. Collins, Jr., and was the original crew to which our crew member, John
O'Neil, was first assigned on joining the 482nd. John had taken the place of Sgt.
Bob Barnes, who had been hospitalized for a time. When Sgt. Barnes returned
to duty, John joined our crew. The other lost crew was piloted by Lt. Warren
E. Bock. Both of these crews were believed to have been downed by flak.

The Following Account of the Mission to Frankfurt, Germany, February 4, 1944, Was Written by S/Sgt. George E. Moffat

It has been a month now since my last raid. I have flown some low-altitude
practice missions to get limbered up once more, but was especially careful of
my hands and feet. They couldn't have been so bad I guess, but they sure hurt
for a while.

I had just come back from the Non-Commissioned Officers' (N.C.O.) Club,
where I had been at a dance with one of the girls in the village named Phoebe,
a nice kid. It was about 10:30 P.M. and I hit the hay.

At 11:00 P.M., a lot of racket awakened me and I popped one eye out of
the scratchy blankets and asked what in hell was going on. Beans said to get my
lazy butt out of my sack, as we were going out to play a little tag with Adolf.
I bounced out of bed happy as a lark, because I hadn't been on a raid for so
long, and I was getting anxious. I dressed quickly and shoved a full clip of
bullets into my Colt .45, and then sat on the edge of my bunk waiting for the
others to get ready, smoking a cigarette and wiping the sleep from my eyes.

There wasn't much sleep to wipe, having fallen asleep only a half hour before. Rats! I thought, but it was one more raid closer to being done, and going home. If only raids weren't so miserably uncomfortable, I wouldn't mind how often I went on them.

The gang was soon ready and we went outside. Boy it was cold and black. Flashlights darted like fireflies all over the airdrome, belying the feverish activity of ground crews preparing our ships. We all jumped on board a waiting truck and bumped our way over to the Mess Hall. Lots of fried eggs were the order of the day and we gobbled as many as we could hold along with toast and strong coffee. We still had 15 minutes before we had to meet in the briefing room to find out what Bomb Groups we were being sent to lead, so we walked over to work some of the nitrogen out of our bloodstream.

In the briefing room we were met by Bill Owen, Mac, Al and Marshall Thixton and a stifling cloud of blue tobacco smoke; we all sat down together, chewing the fat about a lot of things. Then some of the "heavy brass" of the field got up and began talking. We were designated to lead the 390th Group from Framlingham, so after the meeting was over we jumped aboard our truck and went out to our B-17. Only one thing bothered me and that was that we had to fly B-17 #970, and 970 was the same ship Galba was killed in.

We cleaned and checked our guns and laid them in the waist of the ship ready to install when we reached the 390th. We then started engines, taxied out and took off for Framlingham. We landed at Framlingham in about a half hour and a checker jeep guided us to a hardstand, where we were met by five mechanics who said they would take care of everything, except our guns, and we don't let anyone touch those except ourselves. So we got on another truck and went up to a squadron office to find a place to bed down for an hour before briefing at 2:00 A.M. Everyone was still asleep in this outfit. We were assigned an empty barracks and lay down. I had almost fallen asleep, but not quite, when an orderly came in and told us, "Briefing was in 15 minutes," so we got up disgusted, and made for the briefing room.

It was a large Nissen hut and we crowded in. A major got up and the room quieted down. He walked over to the target map and pulled the cover off. There were our little red and blue threads heading right smack over to Frankfurt, a tough target. And those threads seemed to run dangerously close to the red-marked flak areas all the way in and out again. About 600 miles over actual enemy fortifications. Altitude was 27,000 feet and temperature was to be 52°F below. The Krauts would have within striking distance of the target 450 single-engines and 200 twin engine fighter planes, and there were estimated to be a few hundred flak guns in Frankfurt itself. All in all we were not exactly elated over our prospects of returning safely, but I patted Willie on his bald head and said a few prayers.

After briefing, we left for the ship and the mechanics said they had been all over her and she was perfect, so we began putting our guns in and dressing. Take-off was scheduled for 5:30 A.M., so we had plenty of time left even after we had dressed. So we lay down for a snooze. Sure enough, I had not quite fallen asleep when Whitey shook me and said the Red Cross gals were outside with doughnuts and coffee, so for the third time in the night I had been awakened. We climbed out of the ship and ate and talked with the girls for a while and then they moved on to another hardstand.

It became 5:30 very soon, and we started engines. A flare went up from the Caravan and we rolled out onto the perimeter track and taxied down toward the beginning of the runway. We were first off and the engines roared as we rolled faster and faster down the runway; the border lights of the runway increased in speed and finally the ships' vibrations stopped and we were airborne. We formed the group at 5,000 feet and began climbing. We met the 95th and 100th Bomb Groups that made up our wing at Splasher #6 and headed across the Channel toward Dunkirk. As we passed over the coast we got a smattering of flak from Jerry, but no harm done. It was quite light now and the sun was very bright. I watched the ground intently, wondering about the people there and watching roads that were hairlines and trucks that were pinpoints.

We saw Brussels a little to our left and they threw up a lot of junk, but just over the city to discourage us from going there. We had no intentions of going there, but if we had they certainly wouldn't have stopped us, not all of us anyway. We were at 27,000 feet and it felt like it was 152° below zero instead of only 52° below. I was too blasted big for that turret and I was cramped already. As yet we had seen no enemy fighters but we're always looking.

On we went and ran into more flak at Liege. There wasn't an awful lot of it, but it was as accurate as the devil. Those "thumps" were right on us and I heard above the din a ripping of metal. I looked through my porthole out the waist and saw a gaping hole, so I rolled around and popped my door open to get a better look to see if Beans or Sours was hit. They were picking themselves up from a pile of ammo boxes. I got out of my turret and hooked onto a walk-around bottle of oxygen and went over to them. They were okay they said, just shaken up. So I got back in my turret and shut the door after tossing out my walk-around bottle, and connected my oxygen hose to the tank hose. But when I went to take a breath, my mask flattened against my face. I wasn't getting any air! I made a dive for the regulator and pounded on it, but it wouldn't break lose. It was frozen solid. I turned on the emergency valve to try to blow it loose, but no dice, she wouldn't budge. I was seeing bright-colored lights and flashes and I was dizzy and weak. I thought about the door and had a hard time even finding the two handles. They were stiff and I used all the strength I had to turn them. I was nearly out when I felt them give way and I pushed the door open and crawled up. I got the top half of my body draped over the edge and reached blindly for the bottle I had laid down before. After that I don't remember, until Beans was over me slapping my face and I was breathing good clean oxygen again.

After a few moments I had cleared my head and Bill said to stay in the waist until we were attacked by fighters, then to take a bottle down with me to use in the ball turret. I sat on an ammo box and watched as we went onward. It was much more comfortable up in the waist anyway.

A small number of German fighters showed up soon after we entered Germany. However, compared to previous missions in good weather, they stood off watching us. We had the protection of P-51s, which had the range to follow us all the way to the target and return. Since we usually only flew in bad weather, sometimes all of our fighters could not fly. On some other occasions, they would miss their rendezvous point with the bombers. Overall, they were usually there when needed and did an outstanding job of protecting our bombers. Remember, they had from 20 to 50 groups consisting of from 400 to 1,000 bombers to protect. At times this is why an entire group would suffer heavy losses, while other groups, well-protected, would lose none or only a few. I have seen our P-51s fly right through our formation in pursuit of German fighters. On a few occasions, by mistake, friendly fire shot down our own fighters. One time when our crew was returning from a pass to London, we sat down by a flight officer. We noticed he wanted no part of us. After awhile, we asked why? He replied, "your blankety-blanks just shot down the best group leader we ever had." We left him alone.

We reached the I.P. and began our bomb run. We could see up ahead an intense flak barrage. Al alerted Marshall that we may bomb visually if the weather was clear at the target. Marshall immediately got on the bombsight and coordinated with Al. Sure enough there was an opening in the clouds at our target area, and our markers and bombs were dropped visually. The flak was brutal and our waist gunners were throwing aluminum foil out as fast as possible. Maybe the foil messed up the radar of the antiaircraft batteries, so that the bombers farther back in the stream benefited.

After leaving the Frankfurt area, we headed for home and had an uneventful trip back to Alconbury.

The *History of the Operational Period of the 482nd Bomb Group* (Wight *et al.* 1944) reports that bombing results varied from fair to poor. Freeman *et al.* (1990) state that 20 bombers were lost out of a total of 633 that participated. Eighth Fighter Command put up 637 fighters for this mission and one fighter was lost.

Mission No. 12 — Leipzig, Germany (February 20, 1944)

This mission was a classic example of round-the-clock bombing with the British hitting the target at night and the Americans continuing the onslaught during the day. It was too bad that the father of the concept of round-the-clock bombing, namely, Gen. Eaker, was not directly involved with this important mission. Gen. Eaker was to have a special involvement though, as units of the Fifteenth Air Force took part on two days of the strikes during "Big Week."

The combined bombing operations of "Big Week" cost the Eighth 300 airplanes, mostly bombers. More than 2,500 airmen were killed, wounded, or taken prisoner. Almost 10,000 tons of bombs were dropped on the German aircraft industry and ball-bearing plants (Perret 1993).

The Following Account of the Mission to Leipzig, Germany, February 20, 1944 Was Written by S/Sgt. John J. O'Neil

After a break of more than two weeks, our crew was posted "On Alert" on the 813th Bomb Squadron Bulletin Board on February 19th. We hit the sack early, and sure enough, Sgt. Culp came around with his usual curt wake-up call around 10:00 P.M. After dressing, we had our special breakfast and reported to Squadron Operations. It was now about 11:30 P.M., and our assignment was to fly to the 305th Bomb Group to lead the Wing on February 20th. The 305th was a leading Eighth bomb group and was commanded for a period by Col. (later Gen.) Curtis E. LeMay, who was one of the top USAAF leaders of WWII. We arrived at Chelveston about 12:30 A.M., and had a few hours sleep, when we were awakened for more breakfast and briefing.

The target was enemy aircraft factories at Leipzig, which was a major and a very distant city in central Germany. The RAF would bomb Leipzig on Saturday night, and we would follow-up with a daylight attack on Sunday. There would be other targets hit by the Eighth on that same day in Germany, and the combined raids would involve 1,000 Eighth bombers and 1,000 Eighth fighters. It would be the biggest mission by the Eighth in terms of planes and men yet made against Germany. We didn't realize it at the time, but it was to be the start of what became known as "Big Week," because of the intensity and decisiveness of the combined missions made over a six-day span.

We had Al Engelhardt as navigator and a H$_2$S radar-equipped B-17. On our trip to the target, we were not attacked by German fighters. The multiple targets apparently confused the Luftwaffe and we were lucky insofar as German fighter opposition was concerned. Al led our formation flawlessly and avoided flying over German cities and other flak emplacements. It was quite a sight to see the huge armada of Eighth bombers and fighters in the air that day. When we approached the Leipzig area, there were only a few clouds and we could see a cold, snow-covered Germany. Nearer the city, there was smoke rising up and other evidence of the bombing done by the RAF the previous night.

For the past several missions, I had developed a target area routine.

First, I buckled on my chest parachute. There were back-pack parachutes, but most gunners preferred the chest-pack version, and usually only wore them when things got hot. There were many stories of planes exploding, or other sudden mishaps, which happened so fast, there wouldn't be any time to grab and buckle on a parachute.

Next, I put on my regular G.I. steel helmet over my aviator's helmet. The steel helmet could protect against smaller chunks of flak, and was not bothersome.

Then, I put on my flak jacket, which was a heavy pack that covered my front and back, from shoulder to waist. The jacket weighed about 20-25 pounds and was very uncomfortable, but necessary to wear when the flak got heavy. Another mission equipment item that was left up to the judgment of the individual crew member was whether to carry the Colt .45 semi-automatic pistol, along with two clips, that was issued to every combat crew member. Around this period of the European air war, U.S. fighters began making ground-level attacks on airdromes, airplanes, trains, military vehicles and other potential targets. The Eighth fighters would do their strafing on the way back to England after escorting bombers, or as direct ground-level missions. This in effect threw out some of the unwritten ground rules under which the old air war was carried out. German broadcasts to England stated that captured Allied airmen would be dealt with as murderers. Many German civilians were attacking downed Allied airmen, if possible, before German military arrived on the scene. If an Allied airman had a firearm when captured, it could be an excuse to kill the airman on the spot. It was also never clear what a handgun could accomplish for a downed airman in any case. For these reasons and others, a number of U.S. airmen did not carry their Colt .45s on missions.

As we could see the ground, Al and Marshall coordinated to line up the target. Meanwhile, there was a huge flak barrage over Leipzig that bracketed the city. Marshall dropped visually and gave his Bombs Away, and we were in a deep turn and heading for home.

Our trip back to England, though long, went along smoothly. Al's navigation by H_2S was right on course. We saw some Luftwaffe fighters, but they kept their distance, and did not attack our formation.

We went directly back to Alconbury and interrogation and bed. It was the first directly-planned, round-the-clock bombing mission I was on.

Wight et al. (1944) stated that, "bombing results were excellent on most of the targets." There was a price to pay, however, as the Eighth lost 22 bombers and 4 fighters on the combined missions of February 20, 1944.

Mission No. 13 — Frankfurt, Germany (March 2, 1944)

According to Wight *et al.* (1944), the haunting fear of all pathfinder crews of getting lost at night over blacked-out England happened on this mission when Lt. Taylor was flying his crew to Seething, England to be deputy leader of the 20th Combat Wing. Lt. Taylor was reported to have called Seething for directions, and Seething answered, but Lt. Taylor and his crew and aircraft were never seen or heard from again. One member of the crew, S/Sgt. Thomas A. Byrnes was later reported to be a Prisoner of War. Lt. Taylor apparently got lost and flew to Europe and was either shot down or crash-landed.

S/Sgt. George Moffat, who wrote many of the stories in this book soon after their happening, did not record any missions in his War Diary after the Frankfurt Mission of February 4, 1944. We do not know for certain why this was, but suspect it had something to do with George meeting his wife-to-be at Alconbury about this time. Thus, George must have spent all of his spare time courting Phoebe and in early 1945, they were married in Edinburgh, Scotland.

After our raid to Leipzig, where for the first time on a mission I got to use the Norden Bombsight in making a visual drop, I was really getting into it and hoping for more of the same. Then we got the disturbing news our navigator, Al Engelhardt, was to fly this upcoming mission with another crew. Apparently, Al's reputation as a superb radar navigator was beginning to be recognized, and 813th Operations were using Al for special mission assignments.

The Following Account of the Mission to Frankfurt, Germany, March 2, 1944, Was Written by S/Sgt. John J. O'Neil

A check of our squadron bulletin board on March 1st showed our crew was alerted for a mission the following morning. Although I had only completed four combat missions so far, I was beginning to feel more and more like a veteran. I could also look forward to receiving an Air Medal, as the procedure of the Eighth was to award an Air Medal for completion of five missions. Each additional five missions, up to 20 missions, resulted in an Oak Leaf Cluster to the Air Medal, and the final set of five missions, making a total of 25 missions, gave the Distinguished Flying Cross and a rotation home for a 30-day furlough and reassignment. Besides the commitment to carry out one's job to the best of his ability, the completion of the combat tour and rotation home, or the Zone of Interior as the USAAF designated the U.S., was the main goal of most combat airmen, and the medals were secondary.

Before going on missions, I left all English money, bills and coins, in my barracks bag. I did keep in my wallet two "Escape Photos" of me in a civilian shirt, tie and jacket, that were taken at Alconbury. All Eighth Air Force combat crews had "Escape Photos" to be used if shot down, and if contact could be made with European underground forces, these photos could be used for fake passports. The reason for this was that film was scarce and expensive in Europe. In my wallet I also carried a few family photos.

FIG. 8.1. ESCAPE PHOTOS
Top: S/Sgt. John O'Neil, Bottom: Lt. Marshall Thixton.

Just before going on a mission each crew member was given a Mars candy bar and an escape kit. This kit was a plastic case measuring about 6 inches by 6 inches and one inch thick, The kit contained money of the countries we would fly over, but I don't remember anyone ever saying how much money, maps of the countries we would fly over, a small compass, and concentrated food items. Escape kits were carefully collected right after we returned from a mission, so there were no souvenirs.

Almost like clockwork, Sgt. Culp roused me about 9:30 P.M., and I dressed and went to the combat mess hall for breakfast. One little problem I had at army mess halls was I didn't particularly like coffee. I don't remember much in the way of tea being available, although anywhere else in England, tea was everywhere. I recall some powdered milk drinks that showed up occasionally, but these were terrible. The USAAF medical people would not allow GIs to drink English cow's milk, as it was not pasteurized. Although milk was my favorite beverage, in the almost 2½ years I spent in England, I never had a glass of fresh milk. I guess in most cases, I ended up drinking coffee.

We reported to the 813th Equipment Building, got our flight bags and parachutes and were trucked out to our B-17.

After some friendly encouragement and kidding with ground crew GIs, we flew to a 1st Division air base and had a short nap, when we were awakened for breakfast and briefing. The target was a repeat mission to Frankfurt and its marshalling yards. For some reason, I always associated chemicals as a principal target at Frankfurt, but this was not the case for March 2nd. It was still wintry in England and the weather forecast was for complete cloud cover at the target. After losing two pathfinder crews and bombers on the last mission to Frankfurt, everyone on our crew was pumped up to be extra alert on this mission and to make it a success.

We took off on a cold, cloudy morning and after our formation organized, we headed for Germany. On the way in, we experienced flak attacks at several points, and wondered how we would have fared if Al Engelhardt had been with us and navigating by radar. The weather was bad over Germany and this helped keep enemy fighters on the ground. The flak at Frankfurt was extremely heavy and accurate. Our bomb drop was guided by radar through complete cloud cover. According to Wight *et al.* (1944), only 5 of 13 pathfinder planes had satisfactory radar equipment operation, and as a result, various other targets than Frankfurt were hit as targets of opportunity, and bombing results overall were poor.

On our return trip to England, we had one head-on attack by several FW-190s. This really got everyone on their toes and cannon shells and .50 caliber slugs were filling the air. As quickly as the German fighters came, they disappeared, and apparently no harm was done, at least to us. Our friendly fighters showed up at intervals on the way home.

We flew directly to Alconbury and reported to mission interrogation at the Intelligence building.

For March 2nd, Freeman *et al.* (1990) reported 9 of 375 bombers were lost, and 4 fighters of a total of 589 were missing.

CHAPTER 9

AIR COMBAT: 482ND BOMB GROUP (P)
BERLIN — BERLIN

MARSHALL J. THIXTON
JOHN J. O'NEIL

The Following Chapter Was a Collaborative Effort by Lt. Marshall J. Thixton and S/Sgt. John J. O'Neil

Mission No. 14 — Berlin, Germany (March 4, 1944)

After a short rest of only one day, our crew was again put on the alert in the late afternoon of March 3rd for a mission the following day. Little did we realize at the time that this mission would prove to be the first U.S. heavy bomber daylight attack on Berlin and that we would be the first crew to bomb Berlin. For several weeks, Berlin had been the primary target of Eighth Air Force missions, but mostly because of bad weather, Berlin was not attacked. General Doolittle wanted to lead the Eighth's bombers to Berlin, as he did to Tokyo in 1942, but he was forbidden to do so by Generals Spaatz and Eisenhower, primarily because he knew too much about the upcoming allied invasion of France, and if taken prisoner by the German military, could have been tortured and possibly forced to reveal plans of the invasion. General Doolittle reluctantly agreed as outlined in his autobiography (Doolittle 1991).

Berlin was the capital of Germany and the one city that Hermann Goering had boasted would never be bombed by American planes. Goering's propaganda statement may have provided assurance to the German people, but at the same time threw down the challenge to the U.S. Air Force and the Luftwaffe.

Around 10:00 P.M. on March 3rd, we were instructed to be at the 813th Bomb Squadron Operations by 11:30 P.M. After the pre-mission breakfast we reported to the 813th Operations/Equipment area, got our equipment bag, and were trucked out to B-17 number 731, which like most 482nd planes had no name. Our B-17 was equipped with the British H_2S radar and the radome was under the nose of the airplane. For this mission, we flew to the 95th Bomb Group at Horham, the original group of most of our crew. Bill Owen flew and Al Engelhardt navigated skillfully our short trip to the 95th and we landed with no difficulty. Being early March, it was very cold and very dark. We bedded down for a few hours sleep and then had some more breakfast.

At briefing, twenty bomber crews filed into the room. It was a Nissen hut similar to more than a half hundred dotting the mid-English countryside and where, in each, the exact duplicate of today's briefing was being repeated. As the crews took their seats, a low murmuring began swelling in intensity prior to the start of the briefing. Major Jiggs Donohue, of the 95th Group Intelligence, began the briefing. He moved over to the curtains, slowly drew them apart, displaying a map of Europe. The map was covered with long red strings designating the routes the B-17s would follow to and from the target. The murmuring ceased, but was replaced with groans as the crews saw the target for today. The red string stretched all the way to Berlin (R. Bosch A-G Factory).

Major Donohue began, "Boys, this is it. This is the big one. Today, the Eighth Air Force is geared for the maximum effort of the air war. A force of 750 bombers will hit the Germans where it hurts the most, right in their beloved capital. If this effort is successful, it should shorten the war by six months." No one could ever determine how Major Donohue came up with his formulas for shortening the war, because if only fifty percent of our prior missions had been successful, the war should have been over six months ago.

"Latest intelligence reports state that Berlin is protected by 414 heavy caliber flak guns," continued Major Donohue, "however, your routes have been arranged so that not all these guns can bear on you at any one approach." Further low moaning came from the crews. Experience from other targets, with many fewer flak guns, manned by less experienced German gunners, was recalled all too readily.

The Major continued on, "The German Air Force can draw upon 2,000 fighters to defend this area, however, the Eighth 2nd Air Division is pulling a diversionary raid over the North Sea, which should cause the enemy to hold part of his fighter force for this threat. In addition, the weather report states that large areas of Germany are having such bad weather, it is doubtful if many enemy fighters can be launched."

Prayers go up from the crews that for once the weather officer is right. Half or even one-fourth of that number of enemy fighters could make it extremely costly. Major Donohue finished with this classic statement. "Today, Hermann Goering will regret his statement that not one bomb would ever be dropped on our beloved Berlin. Good luck and may God be with you. May I add, I wish I was going along with you on this one." From the back, one of the crew members piped up with, "Major, you can have my place." This brought forth laughter releasing some of the nervous tension.

This was about the fifth time that we had been scheduled to bomb Berlin, but none of these missions had been completed. The weather, missed rendezvous or other factors had caused aborts or the necessity of hitting secondary targets. Although the Royal Air Force had made some night missions, as well as daylight nuisance raids on Berlin using "Mosquito" bombers, this would be the first American bomber daylight raid against this target.

The rest of the briefing continued, as an anti-climax to the all-important knowledge that the target was Berlin. Photographs of the target areas, control points, and our group's position in the 750 bomber stream were covered by the group operations' officer. The 95th position in the bomber stream was extremely good, almost in the center. The group leading the entire mission has the hottest position because it carried the overall Eighth mission commander, sometimes with the rank of general, a fact the enemy knew and tried to take advantage of. The last group of the mission had the next most unfavorable position as the enemy fighters could land, refuel and hit them again. However, it did not always work out this way, as sometimes the enemy would pick out a bomb group in the center of the formation which was temporarily without fighter escort, and attack these bombers with 75 to 100 fighters and inflict severe losses. For this mission, the 95th Group and 13th Wing leader was Lieutenant Colonel Grif Mumford.

The windup of the briefing was the usual pep talk by the 95th CO, Colonel Chester Gilger, a man of few words. "Another great chapter is being written in the annals of the United States Army Air Forces on this day. You men are sharing a part in this history. Good luck and carry on."

The crews left the main briefing room for their specialized sections. The pilots got the latest weather reports, communications procedures, exact times for control points and their individual places in the group's eighteen bomber formation. The navigators made their flight plans and the bombardiers drew their bombing kits and went over the assigned targets once more. The gunners went to the gunnery room to check out and load the 0.50-caliber machine guns aboard the airplanes. The co-pilot, who had a number of side jobs, would secure the escape kits, candy bars, and the extra equipment issued for each mission. Finally, the crew gathered at the aircraft for the final inspection prior to boarding the bomber.

For this raid, a decision was made that changed greatly the course of the mission and the date and unit to lead the first daylight raid on Berlin. At the briefing, Col. Mumford said he would like to use his own 95th lead crew in the lead ship, and have our pathfinder crew fly the right wing or number 2 position in the formation. In this way, our navigator, Lt. Al Engelhardt, by using our radar, could check and help in the overall navigation for the mission. If the weather was overcast at Berlin, we could take over the lead and bomb using radar. Although the command pilot usually rode in the radar-equipped plane (ours) in the co-pilot's seat, and this was the only time the regular procedure was not followed, Lt. Owen was glad to oblige, as it meant we would have Lt. McAllister flying in the co-pilot's seat and able to help on such a long and dangerous mission. The two navigators, our Lt. Engelhardt and Lt. Durr of the 95th, worked up check points for fix information, and the question of what ship would lead the mission was settled.

Twenty mighty Fortresses started their engines and the ground began to tremble and vibrate in protest to the thousands of horses being unleashed upon its surface. The bombers began their slow crawl along the taxi-strips to the end of the runway.

The ground crews, unsung heroes of the war, drifted over to the edge of the runway to watch the B-17s take off. For the ground crews, the launching of the bombers was the highlight of a mission and was only surpassed in intensity of feeling by the bombers returning after completing a mission. Almost all of these ground crews had experienced the emptiness and helpless feeling when one of their aircraft failed to return from a mission. The ground crews did not know the assigned targets, but they could tell the length of the mission by the amount of fuel and ammunition loaded aboard the bombers. They knew this was going to be a long and anxiety-filled day.

Our crew was the third in take-off order, flying on the right wing of the group leader's aircraft. A group formation consisted of elements of three bombers in V shape, followed closely by another element of three bombers, then a high and low squadron in the same pattern. Any extra aircraft would fill in the Vs in the rear elements.

The very bad weather forecast for Europe that day was present in southern England, namely limited ground visibility and a solid overcast at 2,000 feet. Any deterioration in the weather and we could chalk up another canceled mission.

Around the perimeters of the runways stretched the bombers waiting for the green flare that would signal the lead aircraft to start its takeoff. Finally the green flare made a beautiful arc across the hazy sky and the lead aircraft began to roll down the runway. The mission was underway.

After takeoff and climbing, we broke out on top of the overcast at 3,000 feet and assumed our position as the deputy lead aircraft. We continued to circle the field to allow the rest of the formation to get into position. As we were circling, the propellers caused condensation, forming a solid cloud layer around us. Colonel Mumford requested us to ascend another 2,000 feet and continue forming up. Finally, we completed our formation of 19 bombers, all but one making the takeoff, and headed for our first control point.

A total of 750 bombers formed into groups in an area smaller than the State of Rhode Island, which is no small feat. Bombers joining one another in formation was hazardous in good weather and almost suicidal in the present poor weather conditions. We were fortunate that no midair collisions or other mishaps occurred while we were flying over England.

We finally headed for the coast of Holland. This was the last control point to ensure correct position in the bomber stream. It looked like one of those days when nothing was going right. We did not realize that this was only the beginning.

As we approached the coast of Holland, Bill Owen ordered the gunners to test-fire their guns. The bomber quivered as the ten "fifties" opened up. Dust and burnt powder filtered through the aircraft. Our group leader reported that we were ten minutes behind our assigned formation and he was increasing airspeed to catch up. This would increase our consumption of precious fuel and add an additional concern whether there would be sufficient fuel for the return trip to England.

As we approached the border of Germany, Sgt. Aken said on intercom that he received the radio message: "Mission Recalled." We watched as the groups ahead of us turned around to look for targets of opportunity to bomb and then head for home. Soon there were no groups ahead of us and Hoppy Sours in the tail reported no groups behind us. We were sure that our leader would choose a target of opportunity, but when this appeared unlikely, at least, one of the secondary targets not too deep in the German homeland. It very soon became evident that we were going all the way into Berlin, come what may. Mac, our co-pilot, tried to reach the group leader on radio, "Red Leader One, Red Leader One, this is Red Leader Two, do you read me, over?" "This is Red Leader One, we are flying the course as briefed; close up the formation, we can expect enemy fighters any time." This would mean that by the time our formation arrived at Berlin, we would have only 29 B-17s, made up of the 95th bomb Group and others from the 100th Bomb Group, who chose to stay with us.

One explanation given for the lead crew ignoring the recall was that their radio operator had interpreted the recall as a fake radio message put out by the Germans. The group leader and pilot of the lead ship then made the decision to continue on to Berlin. However, the recall was accepted and interpreted as authentic by all of the other bomb groups on the mission, as well as our crew.

Bill Owen felt that Eighth Air Force Headquarters gave the recall for a number of reasons. First, our leaders wanted the first Berlin mission to be a very successful, maximum-effort type of mission and the changing, deteriorating weather put this in jeopardy. The change in winds meant delays into the target, which could translate into fuel problems and a late, possible after-dark return by the bomber crews to England. There was also the possibility of poor weather in England preventing the takeoff of some supporting Eighth fighter groups.

Up ahead, we could see the reason why the mission was recalled, we were coming into solid cloud cover. We began a slow climb to get above the clouds — 28,000 feet, then 29,000 feet, and we were at the maximum altitude for formation flying. We were skimming the top of the cloud layer with occasional peaks of clouds blocking out the lead aircraft. The cloudy conditions made flying wingtip to wingtip extremely dangerous. This of course made us more vulnerable to enemy fighters, should any be able to find us in this weather.

Then, the almost impossible happened, the sea of clouds parted and appearing below, was a large town. We knew we were in trouble and it was not

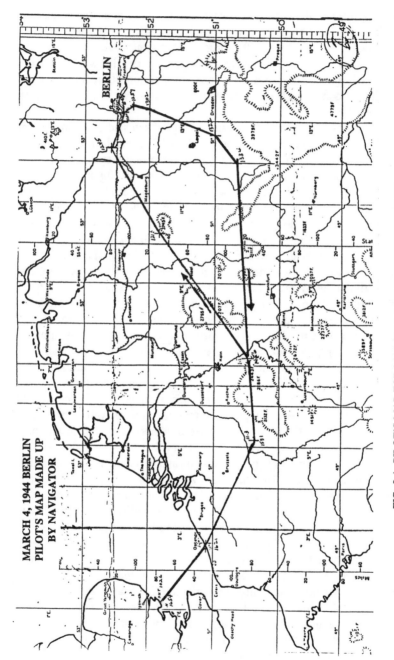

FIG. 9.1. PILOT'S MAP FOR MARCH 4, 1944 MISSION TO BERLIN. The course of the return trip to England was
After reaching central Germany, the briefed course had a northeasterly heading to Berlin. The course of the return trip to England was
southerly and westerly.

long in coming. The Germans opened up with several batteries of flak guns and they had the range. You could feel the aircraft bounce as the shells exploded around us. The deadly pieces of steel sounded like hail as they hit the plane. Antiaircraft batteries consisted of six guns and could adjust their range and bearing with extreme accuracy. This is undoubtedly the most terrifying experience one can have, the completely helpless feeling of being caught in a flak barrage when there is nothing to do, no enemy fighters to shoot at, no bombs to drop, just sitting there hoping the next shell doesn't get you. So we sat there, one minute praying, and always wondering how did we ever get ourselves into this situation.

This flak attack was an early indication that the group leader and crew were possibly not confident in accepting our radar fixes. Al Engelhardt knew exactly where we were at all times, because of the wonderful new electronic invention that could see through the clouds, namely, radar. Most regular bomber crews knew very little about radar at this time and did not believe that it enabled one to see through the clouds. From that point on in the mission, when our formation approached cities, or areas we shouldn't fly over because of antiaircraft gun emplacements, we just pulled ahead and nudged the formation to a safe heading.

Almost as quickly as happened before, the clouds once more closed up and Bill Owen asked for a damage report. The gunners reported one aircraft on fire and going down, with several parachutes blossoming, another aircraft with one engine smoking and dropping out of formation. You noticed the time and what appeared to be an eternity happened in less than five minutes. We took stock of our own aircraft and found several holes, but no vital damage.

So, on we flew, courageously, brave and scared as hell. We wondered if our P-51 escort knew that a small number of struggling B-17s were still heading for Berlin, and whether the 51s would be at Berlin when we got there — or if the German Air Force fighters were waiting for us at Berlin, if it would be another Battle of the Big Horn.

When we reached the supposed Initial Point of the bomb run, the lead ship made the turn to the heading of the bomb run and turned the lead over to us to do a radar bomb run. The time was approximately 12:45 P.M. which was the flight plan time. However, we were by our radar about 47 miles from the actual I.P., and according to Al's map and Bill's notes, 20 miles north of course at this time. This again confirmed our thinking that the lead crew had been navigating without full use of our radar fixes.

We turned our small group of planes back on course to much loud dissent over the radio from many in the formation. Bill turned down the volume on the radio and gave full attention to getting the mission back on track. We flew approximately another 45 minutes to the true I.P. and turned on the bomb run.

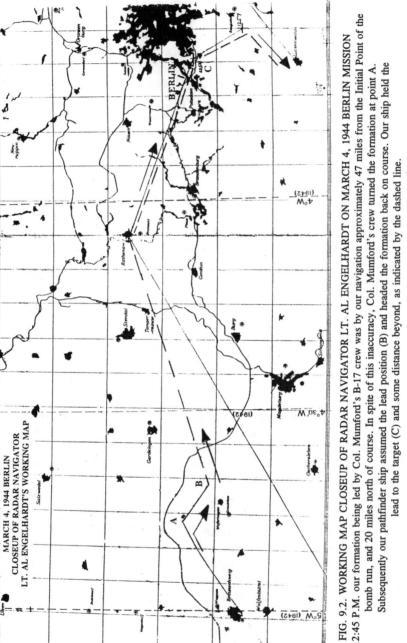

FIG. 9.2. WORKING MAP CLOSEUP OF RADAR NAVIGATOR LT. AL ENGELHARDT ON MARCH 4, 1944 BERLIN MISSION
At 12:45 P.M. our formation being led by Col. Mumford's B-17 crew was by our navigation approximately 47 miles from the Initial Point of the
bomb run, and 20 miles north of course. In spite of this inaccuracy, Col. Mumford's crew turned the formation back on course. Our ship held the
Subsequently our pathfinder ship assumed the lead position (B) and headed the formation back on course. Our ship held the
lead to the target (C) and some distance beyond, as indicated by the dashed line.

Bill put our B-17 on autopilot, and he, Al and Marshall coordinated for either a visual or radar bomb run.

Al Engelhardt called Marshall on the intercom, "two minutes to go, can you see the target?" Marshall replied, "The target is partially visible, bring me in on radar and I'll attempt to pick it up through the bombsight."

At last, we had reached the city of Berlin and began our bomb run. As we approached the target area, we first saw a small cluster group of our P-51s circling overhead, which was the nicest thing we saw since taking off in England hours ago. Our spirits lifted, only to be dashed again. Suddenly there were Me-109s flying the same 4/4 formation as our P-51s. "Fighters at twelve o'clock high — fighters, three o'clock low" came over the intercom. Guns swung into action as approximately 20 enemy fighters came swarming in to attack. Fortresses sent a hail of lead into the approaching enemy fighters, but on they came and from their wings little flashes of light blinked away as they fired their cannons. Don White in the top-turret cut loose on one fighter with his twin-fifties and he broke away, doing split s's down through our formation. As Don fired, dust flew and our B-17 windshield cracked from the vibration. At that instant, the next enemy cannon shell was headed toward our plane. In the cockpit, Bill Owen's hands instinctively patted down his chest and stomach — thank the Lord there were no holes. Everyone was firing and the intercom was full of constant chatter as fighters were passed from one gunner to the next, broken with phrases, "Damn it, I missed him, he is coming through."

Then into the thick of the fight came the bombers' "little friends," our P-51 fighter protection. Don White shouted "watch your fire," as the P-51s followed the Me-109s right through the bomber formation. Fortunately for us, two Eighth fighter groups, the 4th and the 357th, ignored the mission recall and were at Berlin when we arrived. Lt. Chuck Yeager, of the 357th Fighter Group, who after the war was the first to break the sound barrier, received credit for destroying his first enemy fighter on this mission. The fortunate appearance of the Eighth fighters may have been because of the limitations of the P-51 VHF (very high frequency) radio, and the failure to receive the recall message. In any case, most, if not all of the Forts would not have made it back to England without the help of those P-51 pilots. Our crew began reporting the results of this attack: one bomber exploded, two more were smoking and dropped out of the formation. Some white parachutes opened up.

About half of the enemy's fighters circled around for another pass, as we settled down for the bomb run. As the bomb-bay doors swung open, the fighters were on us once more. One fighter passed so close to us that we could clearly see the pilot, and we were spared only because he was out of cannon shells and sprayed us with 0.30-caliber machine gun bullets. As the enemy pilot broke away from the formation, a hail of lead followed him from the ball-turret gunner, and he was reported going straight down. During this time the enemy had opened up with his flak guns and antiaircraft shells were exploding within our formation and their own fighters. Everyone was so busy with the fighters and the bomb run that the flak was almost unnoticed.

In a cooperative effort, Al Engelhardt using radar lined up on the target, and signaled Marshall to drop. He was glad to report, "Bombs Away." The first American bombs were on their way to Berlin, from 29 of the planned 750 bombers, and it looked as if even fewer would make the trip home. But we were homeward bound, thankful airmen, homeward bound.

For all their determination, Colonel Mumford's lead crew did not get to bomb Berlin on this mission, as the bomb-bay doors on their plane froze-up and could not be opened. Colonel Mumford and crew bombed a target of opportunity in Germany on the way back to England.

Our P-51 fighters scattered the enemy fighters, and we became more aware of the flak, which was as thick and heavy as predicted. After the bombs were dropped, we made our turn to the rally point and turned the lead back to the 95th crew. On the way back to England, we were a little more insistent on using our radar navigational powers when needed. It was going to be awful close making it home with not a drop of fuel to spare.

We maintained an altitude of 11,000 to 14,000 feet on the entire trip home. Of the bombers still with the formation, however, two have feathered one engine and smoke is pouring from the engine of a third one. They are having trouble keeping up with the formation, although our indicated airspeed has dropped to 140 knots. It is still a long way home, more than 400 miles.

Presumably because of the extreme cold and high clouds, we did not see one enemy fighter on the trip back to England. Later, much later, Al reported that we were approaching the coast of England. We flew over Horham with the 95th, and then peeled off and continued on to Alconbury. And finally we landed at Alconbury in the dark and cold, and we were tired and oh so weary. As we crawled out of the plane and touched the ground, our legs were wobbly, but we were home and OK. You may vow to never make another mission, but by tomorrow, or the next day, you will be ready to do it all over again.

After landing at Alconbury, our crew reported for interrogation by the 482nd intelligence officers. This involved a complete rundown of the entire mission and all of the recollections of all crew members for details of the mission. The 482nd Group received a call and teletype from the 95th Group, which gave our crew credit for the bombing and the navigational aid for this mission. Col. Howard Moore, 482nd CO, sent a congratulatory message to the 95th BG for their achievement on this first mission to Berlin.

It is difficult to criticize the 95th Bomb Group or its officers and men as their record in the 8th Air Force was one of the best. The decision to ignore the recall and continue the mission to Berlin made by Col. Mumford's crew, was accepted by General Doolittle and other high-ranking officers, and Col.

FIG. 9.3. PATHFINDER CREW WHO LED THE MISSION TO BERLIN, MARCH 4, 1944
Kneeling, from left to right: Lt. Bill Owen, Lt. Marshall Thixton, Lt. Al Engelhardt and Lt. Frank McAllister
Standing, from left to right: T/Sgt. Don White, S/Sgt. Harlen Sours, T/Sgt. Ed Aken, S/Sgt. George Moffat,
S/Sgt. John O'Neil, and S/Sgt. Ellsworth Beans.

FIG. 9.4. PATHFINDER CREW WHO LED THE MISSION TO BERLIN, MARCH 4, 1944
AND SUPPORTING GROUND CREW

A portion of the radome is visible on the left under the nose of the B-17 #731.

Mumford was awarded the Silver Star for this mission. However, it is the opinion of the authors that Col. Mumford's crew, as agreed to, should have utilized the pathfinder radar to a much greater extent, thus avoiding unnecessary flak attacks and waste of fuel, and to ensure finding and bombing the target accurately, which were major factors in completing the mission successfully with a minimum loss of life.

Following interrogation, the officers of our crew were interviewed by a Mr. Wolf of the *New York World-Telegram* newspaper.

The story of the first Berlin mission as reported in the *New York World-Telegram* could not reveal that our pathfinder B-17 was equipped with radar, which was developed for navigating to the target and also the actual dropping of the bombs, since this technology, or any of the details concerning the use of the radar, was Top Secret. Thus, for the record the following story was released for publication in newspapers in the United States without mentioning radar or the pathfinders. This Berlin mission was also reported in the military *Stars and Stripes* newspaper, and a feature article on the mission and the 95th Bomb Group appeared in *Life* magazine (March 20, 1944).

FIRST AMERICAN BOMBERS OF BERLIN
TELL STORY

This is the story of the first blasting of the capital of Germany by an American heavy bomber. The account has been written for NEA Service by the planes four officers. They are Lt. William V. Owen, Columbus, Ohio, pilot; Frank L. McAllister, Omak, Wash., co-pilot; Albert J. Engelhardt, Chicago, navigator; Marshall J. Thixton, Corsicana, Texas, bombardier. At the officers' request, the crew members also are listed here: Tech. Sgt. Donald E. White, North Bennington, VT., engineer; Staff Sgts. Edmund R. Aken, Elkville, Ill., radio operator; Harlen R. Sours, Luray, Va., tail gunner; John J. O'Neil, Malden, Mass., and Ellsworth A. Beans, Pittsburgh, waist gunners; and George E. Moffat, Grosse Point, Mich., ball turret.

An Eighth Air Force Base in England, March 4.— When we got to the briefing room after struggling out of bed at 3 AM, we saw the route mapped out on the wall. The target was Berlin. It was no surprise, because we had been briefed for Berlin the day before but the mission had been "scrubbed" on account of weather.

The thought of Berlin didn't create any special excitement. After you have been flying a few missions you don't think what the target is, but how far. Berlin is a "DP" (deep penetration) raid and anytime you see a DP on the briefing room map you start sweating it out.

Worried about Flak

We weren't particularly afraid. We all had been a bit nervous, and wished someone else had tested out the flak first. But as the briefing went on, we found we were getting good fighter escort and the setup looked pretty good.

We had no idea we were going to turn out to be the first American heavy bomber over Berlin. All we were worrying about was the flak and our four engines. Also for five of the crew this mission was No. 12-B — which is what fliers call the 13th mission.

We drew a good ship. She hasn't a name but she had been on 18 straight missions without turning back and we knew we couldn't let her down.

Far as the Eye Could See

There was a 15-minute delay before the takeoff because of a snowstorm, and for a while we thought we were not going. Then we took off and soon were in sunshine. Even though we see little sunshine in England we were not particularly pleased to see it now.

We were the wing ship and deputy leader of our division. But our division was not the first for when we got over the Continent there were B-17s stretched out in front of us as far as the eye could see. Certainly we never thought we'd end up leading the parade to Berlin.

Weather Turns Nasty

The weather turned nasty. Clouds were piled up as far as we could see. It didn't look as though we would get through. So the Bomber Command signaled each wing to use its own discretion about whether to proceed. Lt. Col. Harry G. Mumford of El Paso, Texas, leader of our wing, decided to keep on.

Soon the other wings started to turn off, heading for secondary targets other than Berlin. Pretty soon we realized we were the only wing still going to Berlin. Then it half dawned on us that if anything should happen to the lead ship, we'd be the first American heavy bomber over the German capital.

Flak and Me-109s

Pretty soon we ran into our first trouble — flak — over a city we had often bombed before. Now we really began to sweat. A little later we reached our I.P. (Initial Point) and saw what looked like a heavenly cover of P-51s. It wasn't until the first few had made a pass at us that we realized they were Messerschmitt 109s. Luckily none of us was hit.

Bomb-Bay Doors Stuck

Just as we were about to swing onto the bomb run, Col. Mumford signaled us to take the lead. His ship's bomb-bay doors had stuck and he couldn't bomb. We hadn't time to realize that his accident made us the first ship over Berlin. There wasn't time to think of anything except making a good run. Luckily we did. We couldn't see what happened because of a cloud below us.

When you're over the target, even in good weather, you don't get much of a picture. There are too many other things to think about. This time it was fighters. They hit us right after "bombs away." Somehow we managed to avoid being hit and started home.

It was a tough trip back. We hit solid cloud banks three different times. For a quarter of an hour at a time we couldn't see more than a tiny piece of the lead ship's wing tip. Col. Mumford and his navigator, Malcolm D. Durr of Alton, Ill., did a beautiful job of getting us back. Credit for the show goes to him.

When we broke out from the clouds for the third time we saw the French Coast. There, waiting for us was our withdrawal escort of Spitfires. A lovely sight.

Mission No. 15 — Berlin, Germany (March 9, 1944)

Once again our crew was alerted for a mission to be made on March 9th. We were happy that our navigator, Al Engelhardt, would fly this mission with our crew. Our B-17 for this raid was equipped with the newer H_2X radar, which was called "Mickey." Major Rabo has told me that he gave H_2X radar the name Mickey Mouse (later shortened to Mickey) when he came to the U.S. in mid-1943 to pick up the first H_2X-equipped B-17s. The Mickey radar had a better resolution, and a range up to 90 miles, which was greater than the older H_2S radar.

Al and I were called down to 482nd Operations early in the evening to receive a pre-briefing on the mission. I was always included in these pre-briefings, because utilization and coordination of both the radar and the Norden Bombsight were important to both the visual and the blind bombing, and there was always a chance and hope of using the more accurate Norden. These briefings were usually short, as we would receive the complete briefing at the bomb group we would be leading. As usual, we took off from Alconbury around 11 P.M. on March 8th and arrived at the 95th Bomb Group at Horham just before midnight. A G.I. truck took us to a barracks where we bedded down for a few hours sleep before being awakened at around 3 A.M. for breakfast and briefing.

At the briefing, when Major Jiggs Donohue pulled back the map curtain and everyone could see the target, it was no surprise that it was Berlin again. Nevertheless the usual groans came from the crews. Just as there were other periods of sustained attacks on major German targets by Eighth Air Force bombers, the period of March 4-10, 1944 could be called "Berlin Week," as there were four missions to Berlin in that week.

The 95th had flown the mission to Berlin on March 6th, and everything bad that had been predicted could happen on a mission to Berlin, happened. Berlin was forecasted to be clear, and it was, and the German fighters made an all-out effort to defend their capital city, which combined with highly accurate flak took its toll on the bombers and fighters of the Eighth. The total losses of the Eighth for the mission were 69 bombers and 11 fighters. The loss of 69 bombers proved to be the highest single-mission loss of the entire 8th Air Force Air Offensive against Germany. The 95th BG lost 8 B-17s and the 482nd BG lost 1 B-17 on March 6th. The pathfinder ship that went down was from the 812th Bomb Squadron, and was piloted by Major Fred Rabo, who was the commanding officer of the 812th. The co-pilot was Lt. Red Morgan, who had received the Medal of Honor for heroism on a mission before joining the 812th Bomb Squadron. Major Rabo had a crew of 12 for this mission, which included General Russ Wilson as mission commander, and a radar navigator, as well as a regular navigator. The briefed target was in southeast Berlin, and Major Rabo was leading the 40th Combat Wing of the 1st Air Division. On the bomb run, the pathfinder B-17 was hit with three bursts of flak. The number 3 engine (inside on starboard side) caught fire and the elevator fabric was also burning. Suddenly, the B-17 exploded and Major Rabo and Lt. Morgan and the two waist gunners were able to pull their parachute rip cords and survive. The other eight crew members were killed. Lt. Morgan was just able to get his parachute buckled and opened in time before hitting the ground.

FIG. 9.5. PATHFINDER B-17 OF 812TH BOMB SQUADRON PILOTED BY MAJOR FRED RABO GOING DOWN OVER BERLIN WITH A LOSS OF EIGHT CREW MEMBERS, MARCH 6, 1944
Shortly after this photo was taken, the ship exploded.
The Mickey Radome is attached under the nose.
(Courtesy of USAF)

Major Rabo spent 18 days in a hospital in Berlin recuperating from his injuries. After being interrogated by the Luftwaffe, Major Rabo was sent to the prisoner-of-war Stalag I at Barth in Pomerania, which was in northeast Germany by the Baltic Sea.

Major Rabo, Lt. Morgan and the two waist gunners, S/Sgt. William E. Wescott and S/Sgt. Steve B. Keaton, were prisoners until they were liberated in April 1945.

After returning to the States, now Lt. Colonel Rabo was stationed for a time at Luke Field, Arizona and flew P-51s. Soon thereafter, he left active military service, but remained in the USAF Reserve until the 1960s. He returned to Chico, California and a career in agriculture. He still (January 1998) lives outside Chico and remains active.

Quite understandably, the 95th crews, and we, were not eager to make a return trip to Berlin. The crews were quieted down somewhat when they learned the weather was forecast to be around 10/10 cloud cover over Germany. From experience, they knew these missions were usually not as rough as those in clear weather conditions.

At this stage in the air war, the Eighth Air Force had developed a procedure where the crews of lead bombers would throw out strips of aluminum foil (chaff — code-named Window by the RAF) over the target areas to disrupt the radar equipment of the antiaircraft crews, and hopefully the aiming of the antiaircraft guns. It often became the job of the pathfinder crew waist gunners to throw the chaff out the waist windows or door while the flak was coming up and exploding all around the ship. The thought of lead crews while throwing out the chaff was — I hope this chaff disrupts the antiaircraft gunners, and helps those bombers farther back in the formation, as it sure isn't doing much for me.

Since our P-51 fighter escort could go all the way to Berlin, the German fighters had to worry about fighting off the P-51s and other 8th AF fighters. Enemy fighters could usually find some bomber groups that were unescorted and attack them, which was the principal strategy of the German Air Force. Although it was not known for sure till somewhat later, the German Air Force was running low on experienced fighter pilots, which helped keep 8th Air Force bomber losses lower than what they might have been. It was evident that our fighter escort was doing a very good job, of decimating the Luftwaffe, as well as other targets, especially the P-47s and the long-range P-51 groups.

The mission started off without major problems. Al navigated us clear of flak areas proceeding to the target. We had some German fighters attack as we moved into Germany, but our fighter escort joined the fray and made it impossible for the Luftwaffe pilots to carry out concentrated attacks. They were able to shoot down a few bombers, especially any bombers having trouble keeping up with their formations. We proceeded on to our target, which was a factory north of Berlin. Al could not pick up the target on radar, so we made a turn and headed over Berlin proper. Other groups had already flown over Berlin and as we approached, we could see nothing but black flak clouds and bursting shells over Berlin. It seemed like all of the 414 heavy flak guns in the Berlin area were firing at us. Sgt. White asked Bill if we were going to enter what looked like sudden death. We all felt the same way. However, Bill continued leading the formation into that black hole. Lt. Engelhardt asked Bill Owen to move our B-17 one degree to the left, which was dead center into the heaviest flak. After entering, we could tell it was just a barrage laid up by the Germans, hoping the B-17s would fly into it. We continued through and were rocked by bursting shells, but received no direct hits. Our group received flak damage, but none of our aircraft went down. We felt extremely lucky and as soon as Al said, "release the bombs," I did, and as I said "Bombs Away," Bill made a tight turn and we got out as fast as possible. We noticed a couple of damaged B-17s leaving the formation, heading for cloud cover, and I believe they made it safely back to England. I know our crew was relieved, and started checking our plane for damage. As usual, we had a few flak holes, but no major damage to our plane. We returned to our base without further fighter attacks and once more were glad to be home safe. The overall losses of the 8th AF on the March 9th mission were 8 bombers and 1 fighter.

Our crew was alerted in the afternoon of March 12th for a mission the next day. However, after going through all of the preparatory activities, we learned that a deep penetration mission to Munich, Germany was scrubbed. The 482nd Bomb Group was relieved of daylight combat operations effective March 22, 1944, and thus the scrubbed mission to Munich was our last call to daylight combat until D-Day (June 6, 1944).

The new assignment of the 482nd was to train navigators and bombardiers coming from the States in the use of radar. The 482nd also was to continue research and development in radar techniques, and to fly single-bomber, combat night missions to Germany until the war ended in early May 1945.

In later chapters, we will cover in detail the radar training program of the 482nd BG, and the major role our crew navigator, Al Engelhardt, had in establishing these training programs. We will also tell the story of the 482nd BG night combat missions.

CHAPTER 10

THE 482ND BOMB GROUP (P) BECOMES A RADAR TRAINING BASE FOR NAVIGATORS/BOMBARDIERS/TECHNICIANS

JOHN J. O'NEIL

The 482nd Bomb Group had functioned as the only pathfinder group in the Eighth Air Force, utilizing primarily radar from the first radar-led day mission to Emden on September 27, 1943 to the last radar-led day mission to Berlin on March 22, 1944. The 482nd did fly a day mission in support of the D-Day Invasion.

There were a number of considerations involved in the decision to make the 482nd a radar-training group and to have eventually radar-trained navigators and radar-equipped bombers stationed at many of the Eighth bomb groups. One was the difficulties under which 482nd crews operated in flying the night before the mission to the bomb group or wing that the pathfinder crew would lead on the following day's mission. For the early radar missions, the pathfinders crews had to return with the bomber formation to the bomb groups they had led and participate in the interrogation sessions. Not until the interrogation was over, could the pathfinder crew finally fly back to Alconbury for yet another interrogation. In some cases, the pathfinder crew might not return to home base Alconbury until the day following the mission. Eventually, the pathfinder crews, after leading missions to Germany, returned directly to Alconbury and were interrogated there. Thus, it was decided that it would be a better arrangement for each group to have their own pathfinder crews and planes and operate from their own bases.

Another important factor was the psychological lift that would be gained by sharing the technology of radar for navigational and bombing needs and familiarizing bomber crews with the advantages of radar. This would be in contrast to a 482nd pathfinder crew flying in to a bomb group base in the middle of the night on a B-17 equipped with a strange-looking radar unit under the nose in the case of the early British radar (H_2S) or a radar dome under the nose or replacing the ball turret in B-17s having the later American radar (H_2X).

A final reason was the shortage of radar-trained navigators and radar technicians indicated that training facilities were needed, and Alconbury with its experienced radar personnel was selected as the location for the radar school.

After March 22, 1944, the 482nd at Alconbury became a radar training center, a radar modification base, and a radar research and development operation.

Eventually a pipeline began so that when new radar bombers would arrive at Alconbury, radar-trained crews in radar-equipped planes would be sent to Eighth bomb groups throughout England.

FIG. 10.1. LT. BILL OWEN AT ALCONBURY, MARCH 1944
(Courtesy of Mrs. Kay Engelhardt)

For many Alconbury air crews, the news that 482nd daylight bombing missions had ended in March of 1944 was indeed welcome. Although an ongoing effort was needed in the start-up of the radar training programs, there was time to think about furloughs (usually for one week), or two day passes to London or many of the other cities and towns in England, or nightly passes to Huntingdon, Peterborough or Cambridge. The GIs in wartime England traveled to every nook and cranny in the British Isles searching for new places to visit and people to meet. In 1944, I traveled to Northern Ireland and explored Belfast and many other Irish cities and towns during a one-week furlough.

FIG. 10.2. LT. FRANK McALLISTER, KNEELING, AT ALCONBURY 1944
(Courtesy of Mrs. Kay Engelhardt)

A respite from missions gave each combat crew member a chance to think over and decide whether to remain at Alconbury or transfer to another bomb group and continue flying missions. The official 482nd position was that crew members could collectively or individually leave Alconbury and join another bomb group to resume combat. Some crew members who were near the charmed 25-mission number, or others who preferred to fly combat, were allowed to do so.

Since the 482nd also had a research and development function, it was not long before a limited number of night combat missions began operating out of Alconbury utilizing single planes. Although there was more or less of a waiting list based on seniority and other considerations, night missions gave an opportunity for 482nd crews to stay at Alconbury and still chalk up missions toward the completion of their combat tours. Later on we will provide an account of night combat missions from Alconbury to Germany. These flight procedures applied to all members of combat crews at Alconbury, including waist, ball turret and tail gunners who were not involved directly in the training sessions of navigators and bombardiers.

All members of our crew remained at Alconbury during the spring and early summer months of 1944. Our crew did participate in the daylight bombing

FIG. 10.3. GUNNERS WAITING THEIR TURN AT THE 813TH SQUADRON
BARBER SHOP
S/Sgt. Roger Moylan (center) came from Chicago
and was a close friend of John O'Neil.

mission supporting the D-Day invasion on June 6, 1944. In late 1944, Bill Owen, Marshall Thixton and Frank McAllister returned to the 95th Bomb Group and completed their mission tours. After completing his combat tour of bombing missions, Bill Owen volunteered to do a tour of fighter missions flying a P-51 fighter in an Air Scout Group that flew air patrols over Europe in advance of bomber/fighter combat missions. Bill was one of the few World War II pilots who flew successful tours in both bombers and fighters. When Bill returned to Alconbury for an occasional visit it was a real thrill to watch him buzz our field in his P-51 fighter.

Our navigator Al Engelhardt was a key person in the training of navigators and bombardiers in radar, and remained at Alconbury till the end of the war in Europe in May 1945. All gunners on our crew likewise remained at Alconbury till the European war ended.

FIG. 10.4. CAPT. BILL OWEN AND LT. MARSHALL THIXTON FLY THEIR
FINAL TOUR MISSION AT THE 95TH BOMB GROUP, JANUARY 21, 1945
(Courtesy of Mrs. Kay Engelhardt)

FIG. 10.5. LT. AL ENGELHARDT AT 813TH BOMB
SQUADRON OPERATIONS, JANUARY 1945
(Courtesy of Mrs. Kay Engelhardt)

During the training phase at Alconbury, Al Engelhardt was moved from the 813th Bomb Squadron to the 482nd Group level as a promotion and recognition of the important contributions he made in organizing and carrying out the actual training programs. In addition, Al participated in the R&D efforts on radar at Alconbury and also was sent to the States with Bob Saxe where they visited M.I.T. (Massachusetts Institute of Technology) Radiation Laboratory to confer and work with scientists there, who were doing the principal radar research for the U.S. and other Allied countries. They also visited a number of U.S. military bases where radar work was being done.

From the report on the trip that Al Engelhardt and Bob Saxe made to the States from July 26, 1944 through September 30, 1944 concerning radar R&D, it is obvious that it was most difficult to obtain full cooperation from the many different groups they visited and consulted. These groups included military and civilians at M.I.T., Cambridge, Mass., the Pentagon, Langley Air Base, Virginia, Wright-Patterson Air Base, Dayton, Ohio, Boca Raton Air Base, Florida, Bedford (Hanscomb) Air Base, Massachusetts, and meetings at Laguardia Airport, New York. The total number of individuals in the States participating in meetings, etc. was 68!

FIG. 10.6. LT. AL ENGELHARDT SITTING, AND CAPT. BOB FELLENBAUM,
813TH BOMB SQUADRON OPERATIONS, NOVEMBER 1944
(Courtesy of Mrs. Kay Engelhardt)

In reading the report, it seemed that in the U.S., several military/civilian groups had some sort of connection to radar, but none of these groups apparently had much interest in pushing forward on radar research to help the air crews who were using radar for navigation on daily combat missions. Remember that the invasion of Europe was only one month old at this time, and the war in the Pacific was 13 months from the surrender of the Japanese.

It is interesting that mention is made that Capt. Chuck Yeager from the 357th Fighter Group was at this time serving at Wright-Patterson Air Base, and was involved in one meeting with Al and Bob. From all accounts, Capt. Yeager made his decision quickly and moved that particular part of the project toward completion.

FIG. 10.7. LT. AL ENGELHARDT ON A WELL-DESERVED
LEAVE IN ENGLAND (1944)
(Courtesy of Mrs. Kay Engelhardt)

As I read in September 1996 the report of Al and Bob on the trip to the States, and the confusion and difficulty in getting things done, I almost don't know how we won the war, but somebody must have been making decisions and providing the overall direction for the radar programs.

I suspect when the trip was over, Al and Bob were looking forward to returning to England and the war, where they knew firsthand what they were dealing with, and must have felt more comfortable with.

Al and others at Alconbury instituted a training program of four weeks in March 1944. The navigator/bombardier students came from existing Eighth Air Force groups and also the U.S. Approximately 75 radar navigators were trained each month at Alconbury (Guerlac 1987B).

The radar training programs and R&D projects including night combat missions, begun in March 1944 were continued until VE Day in May 1945. Around the middle of May 1945, the 482nd Bomb Group began a transfer of personnel and equipment to the Army Air Force base at Victorville, California, where the 482nd Bomb Group radar training programs would continue for crews and B-29s being sent to the Pacific in the air war against Japan. Many 482nd air

FIG. 10.8. LT. WAYNE PLYMALE AND CREW, WHO WERE ONE OF THE TOP
CREWS IN THE 813TH BOMB SQUADRON THROUGHOUT THE DAYLIGHT
BOMBING PHASE AT ALCONBURY
Lt. Plymale is standing at left; T/Sgt. Herschel McCoy, Flight Engineer, is kneeling at right.
Herschel was killed while flying with another crew in December, 1944.
(Courtesy of Mrs. Mildred Plymale)

FIG. 10.9. ANOTHER SENIOR PATHFINDER CREW WAS LED BY CAPT. GURNEY
(STANDING THIRD FROM THE RIGHT)
In latter 1944, John O'Neil was a roommate of Andy Keddie
(kneeling second from right)
(Courtesy of Raleigh D. Lyles)

FIG. 10.10. A GROUP OF PATHFINDER LEADERS HAVING A LIGHTER MOMENT
AT ALCONBURY, 1944
Second from left, Col. William S. Cowart, Jr., who was a pioneer in adapting radar in 8th Air
Force bombers. Third from left, Maj. Roland B. Newhouse, Supply and Engineering;
fifth from left, Col. Clement W. Bird, CO of 482nd Bomb Group during period of radar school.
(Courtesy of Raleigh D. Lyles)

crew and ground crew personnel returned to the U.S. in B-17s, which were
slightly crowded carrying a total of 20 men, but no one complained as the end
of the flight meant home and a 30-day furlough.

Another story of one of our crew members is how George Moffat met a
beautiful English girl, Phoebe Colvin, who worked as a volunteer at the
American Red Cross at Alconbury in the evenings. After dating for almost a
year, Phoebe and George eloped and were married in Edinburgh, Scotland in
April 1945. After the end of the war, Phoebe came to the U.S. and thus
continued a happy marriage that was blessed with two children (Jim and Gail)
and lasted 48 years, only to be temporarily broken when George died June 28,
1993.

Another member of our crew, Ellsworth Beans, and his English sweetheart,
Lucy, were married in 1944.

FIG. 10.11. S/SGT. GEORGE MOFFAT AND HIS BRIDE, PHOEBE,
ARE MARRIED IN EDINBURGH
(Courtesy of Mrs. Phoebe Moffat)

FIG. 10.12. S/SGT. ELLSWORTH BEANS AND HIS BRIDE, LUCY,
ON THEIR WEDDING DAY
(Courtesy of Mrs. Kay Engelhardt)

CHAPTER 11

NIGHT MISSIONS BY THE 482ND BOMB GROUP (P)
MARCH 1944 – MAY 1945

JOHN J. O'NEIL

Although the 482nd had flown night missions to targets in Germany prior to March 1944, the main thrust of night missions began when daylight combat operations ceased at Alconbury in March 1944. The only daylight mission that remained for the 482nd in 1944 was their participation in the total 8th Air Force support of D-Day operations on June 6, 1944.

The objectives of night missions included (1) radar mapping of mission routes in Europe which would provide maps for radar bombing crews throughout the 8th Air Force, (2) testing of modified or new radar equipment, such as Eagle, (3) dropping of propaganda leaflets, and (4) dropping of bombs.

Night missions were very different from day missions. First, they were strictly single airplane missions. Each crew was entirely on its own to navigate in blacked-out England and Europe, defend itself against enemy fighters and

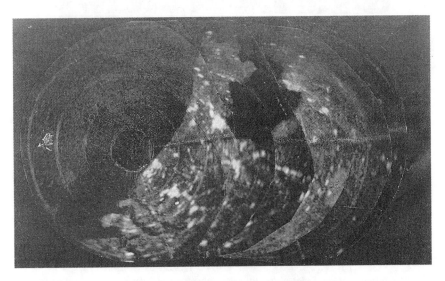

FIG. 11.1. RADAR SCOPE PHOTOGRAPH MOSAIC OF HOLLAND
These scope photographs were taken by the 482nd Bomb Group on May 23, 1944 at approximately six-mile intervals. In the mosaic, upper right center, the darker star-shaped area is the Zuider Zee, a large body of water. The coastline of Holland is to the left of the Zuider Zee. The objectives of the mosaic were to provide a map, which would serve to determine bomber routes, initial bombing points, and reference points lying near targets.
(Courtesy of Mrs. Kay Engelhardt)

flak, and of course carry out the objectives of the mission. Fortunately for these pathfinder crews, the German Air Force was starting its decline in the spring of 1944 from which it would never recover. This important information on the state of the Luftwaffe was not generally known by 8th bomber crew members in March or April of 1944, however by the summer of 1944, it was becoming more and more obvious that the overwhelming Allied air power was turning the tide against the Luftwaffe.

Our crew, represented by Captain Bill Owen and Captain Al Engelhardt, flew the first night missions out of Alconbury, which was due to Al's efforts in the radar school and the overall record of our crew.

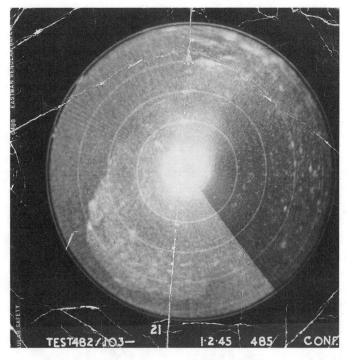

FIG. 11.2. RADAR SCOPE PHOTO TAKEN IN GERMANY
This photo gives some idea of the difficulty of interpreting radar scope information for navigational and bombing purposes.
(Courtesy of Bill Owen)

Briefing for night missions was usually done before 6:00 P.M. so that takeoff could be made before 7:00 P.M. These missions were very long, often lasting about eight hours. To help keep crews awake, the flight surgeon would offer crews a then-new medication which would help them to stay awake, probably very similar to what long distance truck drivers and others take today to stay awake. However, most crew members decided to stay awake the old-fashioned way, namely, be well-rested before going on a night mission.

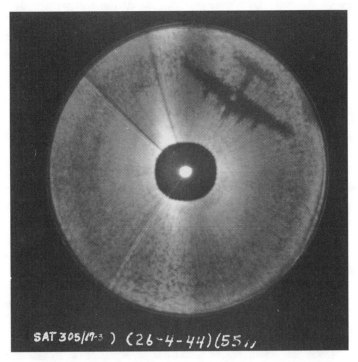

SAT 305/19-3) (26-4-44)(55,,

FIG. 11.3. RADAR SCOPE PHOTO SHOWING THE TARGET AIMING CIRCLE IN THE CENTER AND A BOMBER AT THE ONE O'CLOCK POSITION
(Courtesy of Mrs. Kay Engelhardt)

Each night mission counted as a full mission credit toward finishing a tour of 25 missions. Many flight personnel were able to finish their tours by flying night missions and then go home for a well-deserved 30-day leave and reassignment. As the war ground on in late 1944 and 1945, the number of missions flown by 8th Air Force bomber crews rose rapidly, as sometimes two missions per day were flown. Thus the number of missions required for a combat tour also rose from the original 25 to 30 to 35 to 50 and eventually to an unlimited number. In early 1945 at Alconbury, the word got out that combat personnel who had two years service in the Eighth would be considered as completing their tours with only 20 missions. Needless to say this development had a strong stimulating effect on eligible crews to complete their tours.

Although night missions by 482nd crews were not designed for dropping bombs, I participated in one such mission, on which we dropped a 2,000 pound bomb in Germany. That bomb was the fattest, ugliest bomb and the only 2,000 pounder I ever saw during my stay at Alconbury. When that bomb left the bomb bay, it felt like the B-17 suddenly rose a few hundred feet.

One of the best descriptions of a night mission was written by our Bill Owen and sent to Ian Hawkins, an English author, who incorporated it in the book: *Courage, Honor and Victory*, which was a compilation of 95th Bomb Group missions. Bill's story is recounted below with permission of the 95th Bomb Group Association.

PATHFINDERS AND NIGHT MISSIONS
by Bill Owen

In November 1943 after our first seven missions with the 95th Bomb Group, which included four raids during the notorious "Black Week" of mid-October 1943, my crew and I were sent to the 482nd Bomb Group at Alconbury to train on the Pathfinder blind-bombing technique being developed at that time, using the British "Oboe" and "Stinky" radar equipment.

Within a few short weeks, we were flying to the various Eighth Air Force bases in the middle of the night to join as lead those groups selected to lead the Eighth Air Force, a division, or a combat wing in a daylight mission the following day.

In spite of a shortage of specialized Pathfinder equipment and trained personnel, the 482nd Bomb Group succeeded in furnishing enough trained crews to lead over 80 percent of the Eighth Air Force's missions from early November 1943 to late March 1944. Consequently, the Eighth Air Force actually succeeded in flying more missions during the unfavorable weather conditions of those winter months than it had been possible to fly during the relatively favorable weather conditions that prevailed during the summer of 1943.

By the end of March 1944, each Eighth Air Force bomb group was getting its own B-17s equipped with the American type radar known as "Mickey." This meant the Alconbury Pathfinders (Stinky) were no longer required to fly combat day missions. However, a radar school was established at Alconbury to train the Mickey radar operators before leading their own groups. Our navigator, Al Engelhardt, was in charge of this school. It was decided that radar maps, made up from actual scope pictures, would be of great assistance both during actual missions flown by the Eighth Air Force and in instructing the new crews at the school.

This project was assigned to my crew because, I think, we were the closest to completing our tour. One of the Stinky B-17s was painted black, flame suppressors put on the turbo-superchargers, and a camera — complete with an automatic timing mechanism — was fitted to the radar scope.

The plan was to fly as high as possible (above 25,000 feet) during the eight or nine moonless nights per month that R.A.F. bomber command's heavy bombers flew at that time. We flew pre-determined tracks with the camera taking the scope photographs at regular timed intervals, which enabled a map overlay to be produced.

Flying at that high altitude we saw much of Germany and watched the whole of the R.A.F. missions develop, in stages, through the night. After flying only daylight missions over Germany, it was an incredible sight to behold, and the experience made believers of us all.

With the black landscape below us, any visible light was part of the war: first, the German night-fighter activity, punctuated by occasional bursts of defensive tracer fire, along the seemingly endless stream of British bombers; then the probing fingers of intense light from isolated searchlight batteries; then the marker flares cascading down over the primary target from the British Pathfinder aircraft; then the rapidly increasing movement and activity of searchlights and flak batteries in the target area itself.

As the night wore on, the searchlights, flak batteries, and the raging fires in the target area transformed night into day.

When the German radar-equipped night fighters got among the bomber stream, all we saw was a streak of light, like tracers, then a dull-reddish glow, then falling pieces of burning wreckage as the remains of the bomber plunged to earth. It was entirely different from anything we'd seen during the big daylight air battles that we'd all experienced.

This was a deadly contest of furtive stealth between the hunters and the hunted.

We flew with the R.A.F. during its missions on the nights of 22-23 April to Dusseldorf in the Ruhr Valley, to Brunswick, 24-25 April 1944 and Munich and Karlsruhe in southern Germany, and to Bremen, northwestern Germany, 19-20 July 1944. It was during one of these nights that the German fighters were outlining the returning bomber stream against the light band in the northern sky and taking a steady toll. Even on moonless nights, there is more light than one would think.

(*Royal Air Force Bomber Command War Diaries* by Martin Middlebrook and Chris Everitt reveal that on these three dates [22-23 April, 24-25 April, 19-20 July 1944] R.A.F. bomber command lost a total of seventy-two bombers, or 3.2 percent of the total force committed to battle.)

Being in a single high-flying B-17, needless to say, we were all scared in the beginning. Searchlights would "walk" up to us, hold us briefly, then swing away. During one outbound flight, a high-flying German intruder aircraft followed us back into Germany for some considerable time, but it was apparent that we meant little to the Luftwaffe fighter controllers with all the other activity going on below us at that time.

One extremely interesting night mission was on the night of 27-28 May 1944. We were not aware of the location until the last possible minute, because it was top-secret at that time and had been requested by the senior Allied commanders. Although we'd been briefed earlier to go to Frankfurt, it directed that we were to fly over the south coast of England and take radar-scope photographs of the whole Allied invasion fleet assembled off the south coast. We had all been restricted from flying over that area for some months, but we now had the privilege of seeing a sight, ahead of time, that very few people would see.

On radar, the area of open sea between the south coast and the Isle of Wight was practically packed solid with shipping.

My crew flew again on 6 June, D-Day, and we saw the whole invasion fleet, in daylight, on its way to the beaches of Normandy. It was a sight and an extraordinary feeling that all of us will never forget.

I returned to the 95th in the fall of 1944, flew a few more missions, and after finishing a B-17 tour I was put on detached service with the Third Air Division Scouting Force with the 55th Fighter Group at Wormingford, near Colchester, Essex, from where I flew thirty missions in P-51 Mustangs by the time the war ended. I then returned to the 482nd Bomb Group at Alconbury and flew home in a B-17 after Germany surrendered.

Although the Luftwaffe night fighters became less of a factor as 1944 wore on, such was not the case with the ground antiaircraft fire, which continued relentlessly, along with the resulting flak through which allied airmen had to fly.

I was fortunate in being able in 1996 to interview Helmut Knecht, who was a member of a German antiaircraft crew stationed in Wiesbaden, Germany from January 1944 to March 1945. After a medical examination, Helmut was drafted at age 15 years into the German Army and was assigned as part of the Hitlerjugend (Hitler Youth) to the Luftwaffe as a Luftwaffen helfer with the goal

FIG. 11.4. HELMUT KNECHT IN THE UNIFORM OF THE HITLER YOUTH
ASSIGNED TO AN ANTIAIRCRAFT BATTERY
(Courtesy of Helmut Knecht)

to die within the battle for Adolf Hitler. Within the Luftwaffe, the antiaircraft battery personnel were part of the German Army. The upper age for draftees in the German military in World War II was 70. At the end of 1944 and the beginning of 1945, older draftees were assigned to the Volkssturm and included musicians, actors and others to fight alongside the members of the antiaircraft batteries. Helmut was given training in the operation of the 88 millimeter antiaircraft cannon, the use of a gas mask, firearms, and antitank missiles in case of ground tank attacks. Younger members of German antiaircraft crews had to take high school courses on site and do homework when not involved in military duties. The teachers would come in the morning and teach the younger soldiers history, chemistry, physics, Latin and other subjects that were taught to all high school students.

There were six 88s in an antiaircraft battery. However, the unit Helmut served in was a complex battery of four regular batteries, and thus, had a total of 24 88s. Helmut told me that this complex battery shot down 105 Allied bombers in one and one-half years, which shows how effective these crews were with their 88s.

Helmut's unit had about 30 Russian prisoners of war, who brought the artillery shells from the storage areas to the gun areas and assisted in other duties. At the end of 1944, sometimes horse-drawn wagons were used to carry the grenades to the 88s because of the shortage of gasoline. The 88 cannon

FIG. 11.5. TRAINING EXERCISE FOR GERMAN ANTIAIRCRAFT CREWS SHOWING THE 88 MILLIMETER CANNON BEING SHOT AND SEARCHLIGHTS AND AN AIRPLANE CAUGHT BY THE SEARCHLIGHTS
(Courtesy of Helmut Knecht)

FIG. 11.6. PHOTO OF TRAINING EXERCISE FOR GERMAN ANTIAIRCRAFT CREWS
SHOWING AIRPLANE CAUGHT BY THREE SEARCHLIGHTS
(Courtesy of Helmut Knecht)

FIG. 11.7. GERMAN PERSONNEL OPERATING THE E-METER WHICH WAS USED TO
MEASURE THE DISTANCE TO THE ALLIED BOMBERS, WIND AND OTHER
WEATHER CONDITIONS
The data from the E-meter were transferred to the 88 mm cannon where three men adjusted the
distance laterally and height angle until agreement was reached with the E-meter.
(Courtesy of Helmut Knecht)

FIG. 11.8. GERMAN 88 MILLIMETER ANTIAIRCRAFT CANNON SHOWING
ADJUSTMENT WHEELS AND GAUGES USED IN CONJUNCTION WITH
THE E-METER
(Courtesy of Helmut Knecht)

shells (grenades) were kept in storage rooms with bunkered walls. When duties permitted, Helmut and other anti-aircraft crew members would sit on the bunker walls and have discussions with the Russian POWs. The Russian POWs were good workers and contented with their lot, and never tried to escape.

Helmut was hospitalized in January 1945 for treatment of rheumatism. It was later determined that he had infected tonsils and that the infection was causing the symptoms of rheumatism. He was readmitted to the hospital in March 1945 to have his tonsils removed. The advancing Allied armies were wreaking their havoc, and the electrical systems at the hospital were not working and surgeries were postponed. It was clear to Helmut at this time that Germany would lose the war. He was given a pass to leave the hospital for one night, and instead of returning to the hospital, he deserted and hid out on a farm. He figured he would be taken prisoner by Allied forces if he stayed with his unit, and he didn't want that. On the other hand, he was taking a big risk, because if he was captured by the German authorities, he could have been shot as a military deserter. When Germany surrendered in May 1945, Helmut returned to his home area and his desertion remained a secret.

At this writing (January 1998), Helmut is retired and lives in Florida in the winter and in Germany in the summer.

ADOLF HITLER ERKLÄRTE KRIEG

AN DIE VEREINIGTEN STAATEN AM

11. DEZEMBER 1941

Präsident Roosevelt an den Kongress am 7.1.1943:
Wir werden zuschlagen — und hart zuschlagen. Ich kann Ihnen nicht sagen, ob wir den Feind in Norwegen oder in den Niederlanden oder in Frankreich oder in Sardinien oder Sizilien oder im Balkan oder Polen oder aber an mehreren Punkten gleichzeitig zum Kampfe stellen werden. Aber eines kann ich Ihnen sagen — gleichgültig wo und wann wir zu Lande losschlagen werden, wir und die Engländer und die Russen werden ihm aus der Luft hart und ohne Ruhepause zusetzen. ★ Tag aus, tag ein werden wir Tonnen von Sprengbomben auf seine Rüstungsfabriken, Kriegsanlagen und Hafeneinrichtungen abwerfen.

★ Die amerikanische Flugwaffe greift diese Ziele jetzt an!

USG 5

TRANSLATION

ADOLF HITLER ANNOUNCED THE DECLARATION OF WAR AGAINST THE UNITED STATES ON DECEMBER 11, 1941

President Roosevelt spoke to the Congress on January 7, 1943: We will strike, and strike hard. I cannot tell you whether we will attack in battle the enemy in Norway or the Netherlands or France or Sardinia or Sicily or the Balkans or Poland, or at multiple areas at the same time. But one thing I can tell you — no matter where and when we will attack on land we and the British and the Russians will lean on him from the air without time of rest. Day by day we will throw tons of demolition bombs onto his war factories, military grounds and port (harbor) installations.

The American aircraft attacks those targets now!

FIG. 11.9. EXAMPLE OF AN AMERICAN LEAFLET DROPPED OVER GERMANY
IN PATHFINDER NIGHT MISSIONS
The message in German was on one side, and the American Flag
and B-17s on the other side.
(Courtesy of Mrs. Kay Engelhardt)

CHAPTER 12

THE END OF WORLD WAR II

JOHN J. O'NEIL

The radar school and night mission activities at Alconbury continued through the end of 1944 and into 1945. The Eighth Air Force continued to pound Germany in daylight bombing missions. The rapid advance of Allied ground forces in Europe already showed it was only a matter of time before the complete collapse and surrender of Germany.

Sometime around the mid-part of 1944, the 482nd Commanding Officer, Col. Howard Moore, decided that a threat of German paratroopers attacking our base and airplanes at Alconbury existed and that the gunners should do guard duty around the bombers at night. On the Army scale of duties, guard duty was just above KP (kitchen police) in popularity. The policing of the airbase grounds and installations and equipment was the job of MPs (military police) and other support ground personnel. Thus, the gunners were not very happy with the prospect of indefinite night guard duty of the aircraft.

Worse yet, the guard duty plans were not thought out very carefully or administered adequately, as gunners in the early days were told to go to a certain B-17 and crawl in the waist and go to sleep. For a weapon, the gunners carried their Colt .45 semi-automatic pistol with two bullet clips as ammo. Needless to say, it was fortunate there were no attacks on the Alconbury airbase at this time, as for sure, there would have been a lot of dead gunners. It was an eerie feeling to sleep in a B-17 in blacked-out England.

There was then a gray area period where a more organized attempt was made at full-fledged guard duty with gunners staying awake and coordinating with the MPs. Unfortunately, as would happen, one gunner was found asleep one night on guard duty by the MPs, and was charged with sleeping while on guard duty, a serious offense. I do not recall the exact outcome of this case against the gunner, but it did cause him a lot of trouble, such as reduction in rank to buck private and other restrictions. The event also clarified the issue of no sleeping on guard duty, and after that incident, no further such difficulties occurred.

I will relate one incident I experienced one night guarding a B-17. The MPs issued .30 caliber carbines, which was a rifle-type firearm, but smaller and lighter than the standard U.S. Army Garand rifle. In this later period of guard duty, the gunners would walk around the B-17 hardstand area during the roughly nine-hour stint. The MPs would come out and check each gunner once a night, and bring a cup of coffee. On this one particular night the MP came with his K-9 attack dog. When the German shepherd dog saw me in front of the airplane, he jumped out of the Jeep and started running and barking toward me. I instinctively raised my carbine to a sighting, aiming position and was all set to fire. Luckily for all concerned the MP was able to call the dog off just before reaching me. It was a narrow escape for me and the dog.

Around the end of 1944, Col. Bird withdrew the night guard duty program for gunners, and the gunners were happy and I suspect the MPs were too, as I am sure they never appreciated the amateurish efforts of the gunners into their area of protecting life, limb and property on their base. And there were no attacks by the Germans on Alconbury or any other USAAF airbase in England.

And finally Victory in Europe Day came on May 8, 1945. All personnel at Alconbury and elsewhere throughout the United Kingdom were confined to base. Presumably, the only military to celebrate VE day in the UK with civilians were those lucky enough to already be on leave. There was, of course, much celebrating on base and talking about going home.

FIG. 12.1. JOHN O'NEIL IN FRONT OF BARRACKS AT ALCONBURY MAY 7, 1945
HOLDING THE STARS & STRIPES EUROPEAN THEATER OF
OPERATIONS NEWSPAPER

Soon after VE day, special flights were arranged to take flight and ground personnel of the Eighth over France and Germany to see the destruction wrought by the air and ground war. For me this was a real pleasure flight to Europe, as there were no bombs to drop, no flak guns to worry about, no enemy fighters to engage in combat, and no high altitude and its cold and oxygen requirements to think about.

We flew in that B-17 over a goodly part of Germany, and it was total devastation. The city of Aachen, Germany was completely leveled by bombing and ground artillery. Not even a tree stood in Aachen.

FIG. 12.2. CRATERS AND BOMBED OUT BUILDINGS IN WESEL, GERMANY
IN MARCH 1945
(Courtesy of USAAF via Edward Jablonski and Time-Life Books)

Our pilot, it wasn't Bill Owen and I can't recall his name, found an autobahn highway in Germany, and we flew down that autobahn at 100 ft altitude. Strangely, I don't recall seeing any vehicles on that autobahn. While we were at low altitude, a few children saw us and ran into their house, apparently fearing we would bomb them.

The city of Cologne was unique in that of all the devastation in the city, the Cathedral of Cologne stood out, almost untouched as if you could have walked in and attended a service.

Leaving Germany we flew over France which had spotty destruction. We flew over Paris and saw the Eiffel Tower and Arch de Triumph. Too bad we couldn't have landed and seen the sights of Paris from the ground.

Approaching England from the south, we flew over the White Cliffs of Dover, and then London and finally landed at Alconbury.

Whoever in the Eighth Air Force headquarters thought of sending us over Europe in bombers really hit the mark, because not only did members of the Eighth see first hand the results of their efforts for almost three years, but both the ground personnel and combat personnel had participated in a flight they would never forget.

Word had filtered down that the 482nd would be sent back to the States and regroup at Victorville AAF Base in California. Toward the end of May, the first crews along with ground personnel started for home in B-17s, 20 men to a ship. Girlfriends came to Alconbury and many tearful goodbyes were made. Each man could bring only one barracks bag, or equivalent, home and clothes, shoes and what-all were just left. Almost every G.I. and officer at Alconbury had a bicycle and these were also expendable. But nobody cared, the war in Europe was over, and we were going home. For me it had been almost two and one-half years in England. I departed Alconbury on May 23rd and flew via Wales, Iceland, and Labrador, and landed at Bradley Field, Windsor Locks, Connecticut on May 30th (Memorial Day). Civilians were parked in cars on a road along the runway at Bradley watching and waving at the B-17s, as they landed. Our crew did not fly home together in the same airplane but Hoppy Sours and I were together. From Bradley Field, I and others from New England went by train to Camp Myles Standish in Massachusetts. Then we went by Army truck to Fort Devens, Massachusetts, and finally home for one month.

It was one of the happiest days of my life when I arrived home and opened the door and said, "I'm back" to my mother, father, and two sisters who were still at home. My younger brother was a medic in the U.S. Army at this time. I also had a married sister who lived nearby who had one daughter, Maureen. We all had a wonderful reunion and good food and talked about many things that had happened in the past two and one-half years. As I look back on it now, my father who came to America from Ireland prior to WWI, and was never in the service, was especially proud of me. He would wear my Army raincoat to work and feel as if he were in the military. Most of my friends were still away in the service as the war against Japan was going full-speed ahead. I had a date or two with some old girlfriends, but had no serious relationships at this point.

In any event, the 30-day leave went by in a flash and I reported to Fort Devens for reassignment.

FIG. 12.3. JOHN O'NEIL AT HOME ON LEAVE JUNE 1945 WITH FATHER, JOHN, MOTHER, CATHERINE, AND NIECE, MAUREEN COURTNEY

After a week or two at Fort Devens, I was sent to Sioux Falls Army Air Forces Base in South Dakota. From Devens, we went by an Army Troop Train, which was made up of a number of old coach trains pulled by a steam locomotive. That train was the slowest, hottest, dirtiest and most uncomfortable train ride ever. As it was July, to get some air we opened the train windows and got a little air movement and lots of coal dust. By the end of the day, we looked and felt like we had spent the day in a coal mine. After about three days, we finally arrived at Sioux Falls AAF.

At that time, there were about 30,000 airmen at Sioux Falls, just hanging around waiting for reassignment. I recall there were only about two airplanes on the field, and thus no real opportunity to fly. There was one tragic accident that originated from the base on July 28, 1945, when a B-25 medium bomber crashed into the Empire State Building in New York City, killing a total of 14. Bill Owen knew Colonel Smith who was one of those killed in the crash. To earn one's monthly flight pay, which was an additional 50% of base pay, it was necessary to fly at least four hours per month. The nearest base to Sioux Falls was Sioux City AAF base in Sioux City, Iowa, which was 90 miles away and a B-29 training base. A number of airmen were trucked down to Sioux City and flew in the B-29s and earned flight pay.

For additional spending money, I answered a call from local farmers for volunteers to help with chores on the farm. We were trucked out to a farm several miles from the base. It was an early start as we arrived about 7:00 A.M. The farmer took us out in the fields, and we were shown what looked like miles of oats lying on the ground. We learned that the oats had to be stood up and propped against each other, with the butt ends down. This procedure was called "shocking the oats," and protected them. The grandfather of the family brought us some lunch, and jugs of water from time to time. At the end of the 12-hour shift, we all went to the farmer's house for a huge dinner meal. The whole family was very friendly, and told us if we were discharged from the service to come back and work on the farm. I think, besides the meals, we were paid sixty cents per hour. I worked on the farm three or four times and enjoyed it very much. It gave us boys from the cities a real appreciation of the magnificent job the American farmers did throughout the war, often with a shortage of manpower.

The most important thing at Sioux Falls was to check the bulletin board as countless names were listed daily for shipment all over the U.S. I remember that many airmen were shipped to Alamogordo, New Mexico. I and a few friends from Alconbury, including Roger Moylan, a gunner, were expecting to be shipped to Victorville to no avail. Around August 1, 1945, I was surprised to see my name slated for shipment back to Fort Devens for separation. Although I had many points over the 85 needed for discharge, the war in the Pacific was still to be won, and nobody was being discharged. If I was to start a wave of discharged veterans, it was okay with me. If the Army Air Force felt I had done my duty, I felt good about it and wanted to leave the service and go back to school.

I left Sioux Falls on a Pullman sleeper train bound for Fort Devens. The train ride was very pleasant and the most popular song of the day was "Sentimental Journey." I had to pinch myself to be sure it was happening to me. The trip to Fort Devens took about two days, and I learned the Separation Center was not yet functioning. As my hometown was about 40 miles from Fort Devens, I was able to get home and then report back in the morning.

The first atomic bomb was dropped on Hiroshima on August 6th. A second atomic bomb was dropped on Nagasaki on August 9th, and on August 14th it was announced on the radio that Japan was surrendering. I was at home that evening, and people were gathering in small groups everywhere and asking others if they had heard the news. Everyone was so happy that the war with Japan was for all intents and purposes over. The official surrender document was signed on the battleship Missouri on September 2nd.

FIG. 12.4. COMPLETE DESTRUCTION IN HIROSHIMA, JAPAN AFTER THE FIRST
ATOMIC BOMB WAS DROPPED
(Courtesy of USAAF via Edward Jablonski)

I think most, if not all, Air Force personnel were proud that the Pacific War was ended by atomic bombs that were dropped by B-29s. None of us had ever heard of an atomic bomb, but we felt it had shortened the war greatly, and saved many lives, both Allied and Japanese, that would have been lost if Japan was invaded by Allied forces.

Now the government would really crank up the separation of servicemen, as the military were more interested in sending servicemen home than the servicemen were in leaving the military. On August 19, 1945, I was finally discharged and arrived home for the last time from Fort Devens. Before completing my separation, the Army doctors told me that I had a heart murmur that should be checked later by the Veterans Administration. Needless to say this news put a damper on my happiness that the war was over and I was again a civilian.

CHAPTER 13

A SUMMING UP

JOHN J. O'NEIL

I wish to give a brief statement of what happened to our crew after the end of the war. Of our ten-member crew, at this writing in May 1997, six have passed away. These are (1) Marshall Thixton, Bombardier; (2) George Moffat, Ball Turret Gunner; (3) Albert Engelhardt, Navigator; (4) Frank McAllister, Co-pilot; (5) Ellsworth Beans, Waist Gunner; and (6) Edmund Aken, Radio Operator.

I am happy to say that our living crew members include William Owen, Pilot; Donald White, Flight Engineer and Top Turret Gunner; Harlen Sours, Waist and Tail Gunner; and John O'Neil, Waist and Tail Gunner.

Two of our crew members, Marshall Thixton and Bill Owen, were called back into service at the time of the Korean War, and subsequently remained in the U.S. Air Force until retirement.

Marshall J. Thixton

Marshall passed away suddenly on August 31, 1996 after suffering a massive heart attack. I will fill in what I can of his career after discharge from the USAAF in 1945.

He enrolled in Texas Tech University in 1945 and earned a B.S. in Agricultural Education in 1949. He also had six semester hours of graduate studies at North Texas University in 1969.

As a civilian, Marshall spent two years as a high school teacher of vocational agriculture.

In 1952, he was called back to service in the United States Air Force. In his second stint as an airman, Marshall specialized in electronic warfare, being an instructor and supervisor in electronic warfare school. In his own words, "his last 10 years in the U.S. Air Force were spent mostly in a supervisory capacity involving from 10 to 20 persons, mostly instructors in the Air Force Electronic Warfare Officer Training School." Earlier on, he also served in a flying unit as an Electronic Warfare Operator/Supervisory Capacity. Overseas assignments included service in Formosa and Europe.

In 1968, he retired as a major and joined the U.S. Air Force Reserve. He returned to Corsicana, Texas once again as a civilian.

Marshall and Lorene had two children, Cecilia and William Ray, and one grandchild, Stephanie Renee Thixton.

FIG. 13.1. MAJOR MARSHALL THIXTON JUST BEFORE RETIREMENT FROM
THE USAF IN 1968

FIG. 13.2. MARSHALL AND LORENE THIXTON AT HOME IN CORSICANA
AROUND 1992

Marshall kept active in his retirement years by reading, walking and keeping attuned to current events. One of his main projects was the writing of this book. In 1992, my wife, Lillian, and I visited Marshall and Lorene in Corsicana and we had a reunion after a gap of almost 50 years. Soon after that visit, he told me he was working on a book of his war experiences. I told him I would help as much as possible. Somewhat later George Moffat contributed his War Diary writings, and joined Marshall as a coauthor. As I had experience in publishing, I continued in an advisory role and soon joined Marshall and George as a coauthor. For whatever we have accomplished, Marshall was the driving force.

Lorene Thixton died of heart failure on May 30, 1997. She was a wonderful, strong person, and had helped me since Marshall's passing with the job of completing this book.

George E. Moffat

George passed away on June 28, 1993 after a long bout with cancer and complications.

Like many other 482nd personnel, after returning to the States and a 30-day leave, George ended up at Sioux Falls Army Air Base in July 1945. Bill Owen, who was also sent to Sioux Falls, says he got on a base bus one day and there was George driving the bus.

After discharge in 1945, George returned home to Grosse Point, Michigan. George's war bride, Phoebe, traveled by ship to the U.S. in September 1945, and joined George. When he met her at the train station, she didn't know what to think as George was dressed in street clothes and had a noticeable revolver in a shoulder holster. It was OK though as George had joined the Grosse Point Police Force, and was required to carry his service revolver at all times. George remained a policeman for eight years before deciding to go West.

George and Phoebe headed for California and chose San Diego. For 16 years George worked for Prudential Insurance and ended up as a Vice President. George changed careers again and spent nine years working in the stock market. He then entered the real estate business and for 16 years had his own E.R.A. agency in Los Osos, California.

George finally retired and became active in civic affairs.

George and Phoebe had two children, Jim and Gail, and a granddaughter, Joyce Allison Moffat.

I was fortunate in meeting George at a reunion of the 95th Bomb Group in Reno, Nevada in 1991, which was our first meeting since 1945. Bill Owen and Don White also attended this reunion and we all enjoyed a wonderful few days together. Phoebe Moffat, Eileen Owen and my wife, Lillian, and son, Patrick, and Donna, Don White's daughter, also attended the reunion.

George had suffered a heart attack at age 55 years and recovered. Later he was diagnosed with cancer and underwent surgery and finally succumbed at age 70.

Phoebe still lives in Los Osos and keeps busy by working and sharing with her family.

FIG. 13.3. MARSHALL THIXTON AND GEORGE MOFFAT AT A 95TH BOMB GROUP
REUNION IN ARIZONA
Marshall and George are in the 3rd row at the extreme left.

John J. O'Neil

After discharge from the service, I had one overriding objective, to go to school. I had learned in the Army that without an education, it is difficult to advance one's self. I got a job as a truck driver and started taking prep courses at night to apply to college. In June 1946, the Veterans Administration called me in to check a heart murmur found on my discharge examination. The x-ray of my chest showed a tuberculosis infection and I was sent to the VA Hospital at Rutland Heights, Mass. for treatment. This hospital had only tuberculosis patients and was in effect a sanitorium similar to those institutions run by states or private authorities. The main gate was foreboding as it had a high iron-wrought fence and a guard. I wondered what sort of sanitorium I was getting into. I soon learned that it was much like a general hospital and the patients were mostly WW II veterans and some WW I veterans. There was much time to read and study, and I completed my prep school courses while a patient. Although I spent a long 21 months in VA hospitals, I met my wife, Lillian, at Rutland, who worked there as a medical secretary, and also made lasting friendships with many patients and workers.

FIG. 13.4. JOHN O'NEIL AND WIFE, LILLIAN AT 8TH AIR FORCE
HIST. SOCIETY REUNION, DENVER, 1989

In the summer of 1948 I entered Boston University and graduated in June 1952 with a B.A. in Biology. I continued at Boston University and in 1953 earned a M.A. in Biology. I decided to do further graduate work in food science and technology at the Massachusetts Institute of Technology, and in 1956 was granted a M.S. degree.

I then spent 10 years working in research and development in the food industry in Massachusetts, New York and Minnesota.

In 1966, I changed careers and joined a small publishing company in Connecticut that specialized in food science publications. I stayed there 10 years and in 1976 started my own publishing company, and am still at it today.

Lillian and I had six children: Kathryn, Celine, John, Monica, James and Patrick. We lost Celine at age 5 months due to a thickening of the lining of the heart. We lost Jim at age 19 years when he suffered an arrhythmia and sudden death. All studies after Jim's death were negative for any disease and Jim joined a small number of young people who die a sudden death from an unpredictable electrical malfunction of the heart. Jim was a second-year student in architecture at Catholic University in Washington, D.C., and was stricken and died on campus.

We have eight grandchildren. They are Victoria J. and Gregory C. Ziko of Connecticut; Meghan F., Erin K. and Colleen E. O'Neil of Georgia; and John T., Marcus S. and Caroline R. Habib of California.

Both Lillian and I work full-time in our business. We also enjoy reading, travelling, walking and playing golf.

William V. Owen

Bill Owen flew to the States from Alconbury in early June 1945 and had several members of our crew including Al Engelhardt, Don White, George Moffat, Ellsworth Beans and Ed Aken on board for that joyous ride home. Bill had completed a tour of missions as a P-51 fighter pilot in an Air Scout group just before war's end. Colonel Bird at Alconbury was very helpful in getting Bill returned to Alconbury in May 1945, so he could fly home early in a B-17.

Bill had an early discharge from service based on a sufficient number of points. He returned to Ohio State University where his fiancee, Jackie, was also studying. Bill and Jackie were married in 1946. Bill received a B.S. in Mechanical Engineering in 1948 and worked three years as an engineer in Columbus.

He was called back into service in the USAF in 1951. After the Korean War ended, Bill and Jackie did not plan a career in the military. However, a wing commanding officer made a lasting impression on Bill when he told him, "I am not going to tell you what the service can do for you, but what you and your family can do for the service." Bill remained in the USAF until 1971. He served in the Korean and Vietnam Wars and attained the rank of full colonel.

Bill and Jackie had three children, Ann, Susie and David, and one grandchild.

Tragically, Bill lost Jackie to cancer in 1984. In 1987 he married Eileen who was a long-time friend and widow. They now enjoy a large, combined growing family. Although officially retired, Bill keeps active working on numerous projects connected with family properties.

FIG. 13.5. BILL OWEN AND WIFE, EILEEN,
AT HOME IN INDIANAPOLIS, 1992

FIG. 13.6. JOHN O'NEIL (left) AND BILL OWEN (right) IN
TRUMBULL, CONNECTICUT, NOVEMBER 1996

Donald E. White

When Don finished his 30-day furlough, he was sent to Victorville, California, so at least one of our enlisted crew members made it to the new home of the 482nd BG. When the War in the Pacific ended, Don was sent to Chandler Field, Arizona, where he was assigned as a mechanic to work on B-25s. In October 1945, Don was transferred to my old base, Grenier Field, Manchester, N.H., and was discharged.

Don returned to his hometown of Bennington, Vermont, and joined his Dad and worked on general contracting projects doing carpentry and electrical jobs.

He later worked for the New York Telephone Co. and lived in New Jersey.

Don and his wife, Dorothy, had one son, Jeffrey, who had two boys and a girl.

From an earlier marriage, Don also had a daughter, Donna, who was born in Scotland, and now lives in California. Donna has two girls.

Dorothy unfortunately passed away in 1995. Don has had some serious battles with cancer recently, but has weathered the storm, and is still living in Vermont.

FIG. 13.7. FROM LEFT TO RIGHT GEORGE MOFFAT AND WIFE, PHOEBE,
DON WHITE AND DAUGHTER, DONNA, AND LILLIAN O'NEIL AT
95TH BOMB GROUP REUNION, RENO, NEVADA, 1991

Albert J. Engelhardt

When Al's 30-day stateside leave was over, he reported to the 482nd Bomb Group at Victorville. At the close of the war with Japan, Al opted for discharge and returned to Chicago and the job he had before joining the service, namely, selling newspaper advertising. He also took some college courses but did not pursue a degree.

In 1947, he married his fiancée, Kay, and they had four children, Joan, William, James and John (Albert John III). Jim followed in his father's footsteps and served in the Air Force.

Al passed away on May 18, 1975 from leukemia and complications. Kay still lives in Skokie, Illinois, works part-time, and keeps active with her family, including four grandchildren.

Harlen "Hop" R. Sours

Hop Sours went back to his farm in Luray, Virginia after discharge from the USAAF in 1945. Hop has worked his own farm in Luray since 1945 and now raises many vegetable crops, but specializes in growing chickens. He is helped in all these endeavors by his wife, Betty. Hop and Betty had two sons and a daughter. Unfortunately, one son was killed in an automobile accident while still in his twenties. Pam is married and lives in Luray. Their other son is married and works on the farm with Hop.

In August 1992, my wife, Lillian, and I met Hop, Betty and Pam and her husband at a reunion of the 95th Bomb Group in Newton, Massachusetts. We had a wonderful time together for a few days. Hop over the years had changed from a rather quiet young man to a sort of a Will Rogers' philosopher, ready

FIG. 13.8. HARLEN "HOP" SOURS AND WIFE, BETTY, AT 95TH BOMB GROUP REUNION, NEWTON, MASS., 1992

to discuss a wide variety of subjects. Hop told me that he has never been on another airplane flight since we landed on May 30, 1945 at Bradley Field, Connecticut on the last leg of our trip home from England.

Frank L. McAllister

Frank had finished his tour of missions at the 95th Bomb Group in early 1945 and returned to the States. About all we know about Frank is that after the war and his discharge, he returned to his home area in Washington State. Apparently, Frank developed medical problems and passed away at a fairly young age.

Ellsworth A. Beans

Ellsworth returned to the Pittsburgh area after being discharged from the service. He and his English war-bride, Lucy, lived and worked in Pittsburgh after the war, and both are deceased now.

Edmund R. Aken

Ed returned to Cartersville, Illinois after discharge from the service. The last news we had of Ed is that around 1991 he was in a nursing home, and we now believe he has passed away.

The U.S. Army Air Forces played a very important role in the overall U.S. military effort in World War II. I believe one reason for this success was the "Team Effort" concept that the USAAF stressed in getting the job done. Although some airmen felt it was a special type of propaganda, the repetitive reminders eventually sunk in and established goals for both officers and men.

In my service period of slightly over four years, I spent approximately half of that time as a ground crew member (medic) and half as an air crew member. When I first reported to the 482nd Bomb Group as an aerial gunner, I and another gunner, Herschel McCoy, were assigned to a ground crew barracks. Most of the personnel in this barracks were radar mechanics, but we also had airplane mechanics, a cryptographer, an armorer, a supply person, and a few occupational specialties I can't recall now. Some radar technicians flew as observers on training missions in England, and on a few occasions flew on actual combat missions.

These experiences allowed me to see firsthand the tremendous job the ground personnel did to "Keep 'Em Flying." I also observed on a number of occasions the loyalty and respect that ground crew had for flying personnel. I doubt if any gunner on a mission in the whole Eighth Air Force was more anxiously awaited to return safely, than Herschel and I to our ground crew barracks.

I spent about a year in that barracks, and was really sorry to move into an air crew barracks when space was available and I was forced to move.

I would like to make a few comments on WW II. In comparison to the Korean War and the Vietnam War, WW II is often given as an example of a war in which members of the U.S. military were highly motivated and patriotic. It is of course true that after Pearl Harbor, most of the U.S. was completely united with the goal of winning the war. Members of the government, industry, academia, media, Hollywood, agriculture and the man in the street worked together to win the war. However, I can't say that the average serviceman, whether combat or non-combatant, was serving because he was patriotic. Everybody knew there was a war to win and they had a job to do. There were no serious discussions on the politics of the war that I recall. The same could be said for most of the men I saw in combat. They did not say they were willing to die for patriotic reasons. One way or another they had volunteered for combat in the Army Air Forces, whether for a desire for adventure or the lure of flying. For me, it was probably a combination of the above two reasons. But air combat was a frightening experience, and many a time I asked myself on a mission, what was I doing in this job. Maybe in some way I was helping to protect the Jewish girl I used to date or other Jewish friends, or oppressed groups. And another answer was, it was a job and I, one way or another, had that job. There was a commitment to one's self, to fellow crew members, your squadron, and to one's family and friends that as long as your mental and physical health allowed, you were going to fly combat missions until you completed your tour or you were shot down.

If I had been in the Korean War, Vietnam War or Gulf War, I believe I would have served and felt the same, just as Bill Owen and Marshall Thixton did in the Korean and Vietnam Wars. All wars are failures by both sides to find a better way to solve the problem. I remember the first Italian Prisoner of War I saw in England, and I thought, why should he want to kill me or I want to kill him. I couldn't come up with an answer.

Unfortunately, I must say that I don't think the generation of the Vietnam War era would have wanted to fight in WW II anymore than they wanted to fight in Vietnam. There was that much change in values, ideals and commitment in the roughly 25 years from 1940 through the mid-1960s. To those who think that World War II was different than other wars, I recommend they think about the message in the line from the movie, *All Quiet on the Western Front*, "The Living Get the Iron Cross; The Wounded Get The Red Cross; The Dead Get The Wooden Cross; And They All Get The Double Cross."

BIBLIOGRAPHY

ANDERSON, C.E. and HAMELIN, J.P. 1990. To Fly and Fight — Memoirs of a Triple Ace. St. Martin's Press, New York.

ARMSTRONG, R.W. and STONE, K. 1991. USA: The Hard Way — An Autobiography of a B-17 Crew Member. Quail House Publishing Co., Orange County, Calif.

ATKINS, E.R. 1996. Fighting Scouts of the Eighth Air Force. Scouting Force Association, Arlington, Texas.

BAUMBACK, W. 1949. Broken Swastika — The Defeat of the Luftwaffe. Dorset Press, Div. of Marboro Books Corp., New York.

BENDINER, E. 1980. The Fall of Fortresses. G.P. Putnam's Sons, New York.

BENNETT, D.C.T. 1988. Pathfinder — A War Autobiography. Goodall Publications Ltd., London.

BIRDSALL, S. 1973. Log of the Liberators. Doubleday & Company, Garden City, N.Y.

BIRDSALL, S. and FREEMAN, R.A. 1994. Claims to Fame — The B-17 Flying Fortress. Arms and Armour Press, London.

BOWMAN, M.W. 1944. Great American Air Battles of World War II. Barnes & Noble, New York.

BOWMAN, M.W. 1997. USAAF Handbook, 1939-1945. Stackpole Books, Mechanicsburg, Penn.

BUDERI, R. 1996. The Invention That Changed the World. Simon and Shuster, New York.

CAINE, P.D. 1995. Spitfires, Thunderbolts, and Warm Beer: An American Fighter Pilot Over Europe. Brassey's, Washington, D.C.

CALDWELL, D.L. 1991. J.G. 26 — Top Guns of the Luftwaffe. Orion Books, Div. of Crown Publishers, New York.

CARTY, P. 1990. Secret Squadrons of the Eighth. Specialty Press, Stillwater, Minn.

COFFEY, T.M. 1986. Iron Eagle — The Turbulent Life of General Curtis LeMay. Crown Publishers, New York.

COMMAGER, H.S. 1945. The Story of the Second World War. Brassey's Book Orders, c/o Macmillan Publishing Co., Riverside, N.J.

CRAVEN, W.F. and CATE, J.L. 1948. The Army Air Forces in World War II, Vols. 1-7. University of Chicago Press, Chicago.

CROSBY, H.H. 1993. A Wing and A Prayer. Harper Collins Publishers, New York.

DOOLITTLE, J.H. and GLINES, C.V. 1991. I Could Never Be So Lucky Again. Bantam Books, New York.

ETHELL, J.L. and PRICE, A. 1989. Target Berlin: Mission 250 — 6 March 1944. Arms and Armour Press, London.

FLETCHER, E. 1992. The Lucky Bastard Club: A B-17 Pilot in Training and in Combat, 1943-45. Univ. of Washington Press, Seattle, Wash.

FREEMAN, R.A. 1989. The Mighty Eighth (A History of the Units, Men and Machines of the U.S. 8th Air Force). Orion Books, Division of Crown Publishers, New York.

FREEMAN, R.A. 1991. Mighty Eighth War Manual. Motorbooks International Publishers & Wholesalers, Osceola, Wis.

FREEMAN, R.A. 1992A. Airfields of the Eighth — Then and Now. Battle of Britain Prints International Ltd., London.

FREEMAN, R.A. 1992B. The Mighty Eighth in Color. Specialty Press Publishers and Wholesalers, Stillwater, Minn.

FREEMAN, R.A. 1996. The Mighty Eighth in Art. Arms and Armour Press, London.

FREEMAN, R.A., CROUCHMAN, A. and MASLEN, V. 1990. Mighty Eighth War Diary. Motorbooks International, Publishers and Wholesalers, Osceola, Wis.

GLINES, C.V. 1988. The Doolittle Raid. Orion Books, Div. of Crown Publishers, New York.

GUERLAC, H.E. 1978A. Radar in World War II, Vol. 8, Sections A-C. American Institute of Physics (Tomash Publishers), New York.

GUERLAC, H.E. 1978B. Radar in World War II, Vol. 8, Sections D-E. American Institute of Physics (Tomash Publishers), New York.

HASTINGS, M. 1979. Bomber Command. Touchstone, Simon & Schuster, New York.

HAWKINS, I.L. 1984. The Munster Raid: Bloody Skies Over Germany. Tab/Aero Books, Blue Ridge, Summit, Penn.

HAWKINS, I.L. 1987. Courage—Honor—Victory. Hunter Publishing Co., Winston-Salem, N.C.

HAWKINS, I.L. 1990. B-17s Over Berlin: Personal Stories from the 95th Bomb Group (H). Brassey's (US), McLean, Va.

HUTTON, S.M. 1994. Personal communication.

JABLONSKI, E. 1965. Flying Fortress. Doubleday & Company, Garden City, N.Y.

JABLONSKI, E. 1971. Airwar: Outraged Skies: Wings of Fire. Doubleday & Company, Garden City, N.Y.

KAPLAN, P. and SMITH, R.A. 1983. One Last Look. Abbeville Press, New York.

LeMAY, C.E. and YENNE, B. 1988. Superfortress — The B-29 and American Air Power. McGraw-Hill Book Company, New York.

McFARLAND, S.L. 1995. America's Pursuit of Precision Bombing, 1910-1945. Smithsonian Institution Press, Washington, D.C.

METS, D. 1988. Master of Airpower — General Carl A. Spaatz. Presidio Press, Novato, Calif.

MIDDLEBROOK, M. 1984. The Battle of Hamburg. Penguin Books, London.

MIDDLEBROOK, M. 1985. The Schweinfurt-Regensburg Mission: American Raids on 17 August 1943. Penguin Books, London.

MIDDLEBROOK, M. 1990. The Berlin Raids — R.A.F. Bomber Command Winter 1943-44. Penguin Books, London.

PARNELL, B. 1987. Carpetbaggers: America's Secret War in Europe. Eakin Press, Austin, Texas.

PARTON, J. 1986. Air Force Spoken Here. Adler and Adler, Publishers, Bethesda, Md.

PERRET, G. 1993. Winged Victory: The Army Air Forces in World War II. Random House, New York.

PAPE, R.A. 1996. Bombing to Win — Air Power and Coercion in War. Cornell University Press, Ithaca, N.Y.

PRICE, A. 1984; 1989. The History of U.S. Electronic Warfare, Vols. I and II. The Association of Old Crows, Arlington, Va.

ROANE, O.D. 1995. A Year in the Life of a Cowboy with the Bloody 100th. CTR Enterprises, Houston, Texas.

SMALLWOOD, J.W., JR. 1992. Tomlin's Crew: A Bombardier's Story. Sunflower University Press, Manhattan, Kan.

SWAYZE, J. 1993. Sporty Course — Memoirs of a World War II Bomber Pilot. Sunflower University Press, Manhattan, Kan.

THOMAS, G. and WITTS, M.M. 1990. Ruin from the Air — The Enola Gay's Atomic Mission to Hiroshima. Scarborough House/Publishers, Chelsea, MI.

THOMPSON, S.A. 1990. Final Cut — The Post-War B-17 Flying Fortress: The Survivors. Pictorial Histories Publishing Company, Missoula, Mont.

TOLIVER, R.F. and CONSTABLE, T.J. 1990. Fighter General: The Life of Adolf Galland. AmPress Publishing, Zephyr Cove, Nevada.

WATRY, C.A. and HALL, D.L. 1986. Aerial Gunners: The Unknown Aces of World War II. California Aero Press, Carlsbad, Calif.

WIGHT, I.E., DAVIS, J.M., EARLE, F.A., ROLL, C.V., HORNE, J.W., CRAMPTON, H.L. and DAVIS, B. 1944. History of the Operational Period of the 482nd Bombardment Group (P), Aug. 20, 1943-March 31, 1944. USAAF Unpublished.

WOOLNOUGH, J.H. 1978. The 8th Air Force Album. 8th AF News, Hollywood, Fla.

YEAGER, C. and JANOS, L. 1986. Yeager — An Autobiography. Bantam Books, New York.

ZEMKE, H. and FREEMAN, R.A. 1989. Zemke's Wolf Pack. Crown Publishers, New York.

ZEMKE, H. and FREEMAN, R.A. 1991. Zemke's Stalag — The Final Days of World War II. Smithsonian Institution Press, Washington, D.C.

INDEX